How To Create Cultures:

How Climate Influences The Cultures You Create, A Reference For Writers, Gamers And Amateur Geographers!

AMY LAURENS

OTHER WORKS

SANCTUARY SERIES
Where Shadows Rise
Through Roads Between
When Worlds Collide
The Complete Sanctuary Series

KADITEOS: MERCURY SERIES
How Not To Acquire A Castle
How Not To Ring The Hero's Bell (2019)
How Not To Take Over The World (2019/20)

NON-FICTION
The 32 Worst Mistakes People Make About Dogs
How To Plan A Pinterest-Worthy Party Without Dying or Losing Your Chill

INKPRINT WRITERS
How To Write Dogs
How To Theme
How To Create Cultures
How To Create Life (2019)
How To Map (2019)

Find other works by the author at
http://www.amylaurens.com/books/

How To Create Cultures:

How Climate Influences The Cultures You Create, A Reference For Writers, Gamers And Amateur Geographers!

AMY LAURENS

Inkprint PRESS
www.inkprintpress.com

Copyright © 2019 Amy Laurens

All rights reserved. No part of this book may be reproduced in any form or by any electronic or mechanical means, including information storage and retrieval systems, without permission in writing from the publisher, except by a reviewer, who may quote brief passages in a review.

Print ISBN: 978-1-925825-87-9
eBook ISBN: 9781386647782

www.inkprintpress.com

National Library of Australia Cataloguing-in-Publication Data
Laurens, Amy 1985 –
How To Create Cultures
252 p.
ISBN: 978-1-925825-87-9
Inkprint Press, Canberra, Australia
　　1. Language Arts & Disciplines—Writing—Fiction Writing 2. Social Science—Anthropology—Cultural & Social 3. Social Science—Demography

First Edition: January 2019

Summary: Learn how climate and access to technology impact the fictional cultures you create.

Cover design © Inkprint Press.

CONTENTS

Acknowledgements
Introduction											1

PART ONE: THE BIOMES								4
Tropical Forests										10
Tropical Savannahs									26
Deserts													38
Temperate Climates									50
Cold Forests											69
Tundras													80
Water Biomes											94
    Ponds and Lakes								96
    Rivers and Streams							102
    Wetlands										106
    Estuaries										111
    Oceans											115
    Coral Reefs									124
Moving Forward										128

PART TWO: TECHNOLOGY AND CULTURE		130
Stage 1													140
Stage 2													160
Stage 3													180
Stage 4													203
A Note on Religion									222

Conclusion												225
References

ACKNOWLEDGEMENTS

How To Create Cultures is a stand-alone section from my non-fiction 'magnus opus', *From The Ground Up*. Writing this book (both as in *How To Create Cultures* and *From The Ground Up* as a whole) has been a massive, massive journey. I owe extreme thanks to everyone who's been even tangentially involved, but without Krista D. Ball, I would never have moved past this vague, nebulous idea that I could one day put my love of demographic geography to use and talk about the ways that climate impacts culture. Krista was the one who encouraged me to write this up as a proper proposal and submit it, thereby overcoming the massive writing block I'd been experiencing. I'd actually quit writing entirely, largely because of postnatal depression, and this project—and Krista—got me writing again. With all my heart, *thank you*.

I also owe massive thanks to Margaret, who spent hours combing over my early drafts, suggesting massive restructurings that have made this whole mess comprehensible for people outside my brain. Both she, and also Jason, deserve so much gratitude for their assistance with those early edits.

And finally, immense thanks to Lynne McInnes, Cadena Mckenzie, and Katje: this book would have been infinitely poorer without you, and far more riddled with errors. Thank you so, so much for your generosity and time in helping me to get as much of this right as I could. Any remaining errors are, of course, all mine.

Of course, none of this would have happened in the first place had my Dad not instilled a love of maps and geography in me early on in the first place: our huge, gold family atlas will always hold a special place in my heart. Thank you so very, very much.

INTRODUCTION

Let's be honest: there is a *lot* of information out there in the great cobwebby beyond about how to create cultures. And a lot of it begins with checklists: what do your people eat, what sort of government do they have, what kind of clothes do they wear, what level of tech do they possess, etc?

Now, while I have nothing against a good checklist, approaching your culture creation thusly is somewhat misleading. It rather implies that culture is a kind of mix-and-match grab-bag: a style of government from over here, a style of clothing from over there; a little of this cuisine, a little of that technology.

And while this kind of approach can certainly generate some *creative* results, a lot of the time, the results it produces don't intuitively work. Why? Because cultures are born from their environments.

We know intuitively that polyester is a bad idea in the tropics; and maybe we can even see that meat-heavy diets are linked to colder climes, while diets rich in tropical fruits are, well, obviously tropical.

But what about things like art? What about family, and marriage, and the economy? What about the type of government?

Believe it or not, these kinds of things are influenced by a culture's environment too, as well as by the culture's level of industrialisation. And this book is going to tell you exactly how.

There are two parts to *How To Create Cultures*. In Part One, I will walk you through the ten major land-based climate zones, as well as the six major aquatic environments. For each we're going to explore how that particular type of environment—each *biome*—impacts a culture's:

- Food
- Clothing style
- Shelter style
- Attitudes towards marriage and family
- Economic development
- Approach to health and medicine
- Style of art and leisure

Of course, some biomes impact culture more than others. There are some biomes, for example, that support such wide ranges of cultural behaviour and beliefs (about marriage and the family in particular) that it's impossible to draw generalisations. In these instances, some of the above sections have been left out. If a section is missing, assume that you're safe to choose any option and still have it sit plausibly within the environment of your culture.

Also, the biome of the culture isn't the only thing that impacts how it develops. Technology plays a major role in shaping societies; the more complex the technology is, the more influential it is over the culture, reducing the influence of the culture's physical environment.

So, in Part Two, we will explore a concept called the demographic transition. Now, these are more what you'd call 'guidelines' than actual rules.

The demographic transition isn't prescriptive, it isn't compulsory, and it's certainly messy, complex and sometimes outright problematic in its application to real life. But when you're looking to create your own plausible culture, it provides an excellent reference point to think about how different levels of technology can impact the development and values of a culture.

And now that that's sorted, let's turn to Part One…

PART ONE: THE BIOMES

Before we get to the demographic transition though, let's lay the groundwork.

(We're about to refresh our collective memories about what the different biomes are. We're literally figuring out what the ground the culture lives on looks like. Laying the groundwork, right? Ha!)

First of all, what's a biome? (BYE-ome)

'Biome' is the scientific word for the combined plant and animal life that exists in a particular location.

The key, though, is that this plant-and-animal life is a distinct community that has formed in response to the climate of the area. It's different to the plant-and-animal life in neighbouring areas, because the long-term weather patterns—the climate—is different.

You can have small biomes (microbiomes), as specific as the microbiome of your hands or your stomach (each containing different plant-and-animal life at a microscopic level that have adapted to live in those different 'climates'), and you can have large biomes, such as a desert or tropical rainforest.

PART ONE: THE BIOMES

As I mentioned before, in this book we will look at ten different terrestrial (land-based) biomes, and six aquatic (water-based) ones. Here's a quick summary of them before we get into detail:

TROPICAL BIOMES

Tropical climates receive large amounts of rainfall throughout the year and have high average temperatures. They are found around the equator and in tropical regions, and can be further categorised as either having year-round rainfall with no dry season, a short dry season with fairly continuous rain during the rest of the year, or tropical temperatures but semi-arid levels of rainfall (i.e. not much).
- Tropical Rain Forests
- Tropical Dry Forests
- Tropical Savannahs

DESERT BIOMES

Deserts are climate that form in areas with very little rainfall and a huge variation between night-time and day-time temperatures. Dry climates can be semi-arid/steppe, or arid/desert.
- Deserts
- Semi-arid or steppe regions

PART ONE: THE BIOMES

TEMPERATE BIOMES

Temperate climates generally have warm, dry summers and cool, wet winters. There is a lot of variation across these climates, mostly influenced by how close the area is to the ocean. This category includes subtropical climates (which, rather than having dry summers and wet winters, can have year-round rainfall), Mediterranean climates, and most coastal regions.

- Temperate Forests (regular rainfall year-round)
- Temperate Woodlands (rain concentrated at a particular time of year, usually winter or summer)
- Temperate Grasslands (less rainfall than temperate woodlands or tropical savannahs)

CONTINENTAL BIOMES

Continental (cold forest) climates are found only in the interior of large continents in the northern hemisphere in our world. They have lower rainfall than other temperate climates, but still more than desert climates.

- Boreal Forests
- North-west Coniferous Forests

PART ONE: THE BIOMES

TUNDRA BIOMES

Cold climates are, as the name suggests, climates where temperatures are above freezing for less than four months of the year. They are also known as polar climates, and much of their ground is permanently frozen solid.
- Tundra

WATER BIOMES

As well as these terrestrial biomes, we're also going to look at the following aquatic biomes:
- Ponds and lakes (standing fresh water)
- Rivers and streams (running fresh water)
- Wetlands (such as bogs or swamps)
- Estuaries (where fresh and salt water mix)
- Oceans (large bodies of salt water)
- Coral Reefs (a specific part of ocean biomes)

Somewhat obviously, the aquatic biomes have more to do with the amount and type of water available than with climate or weather patterns. You can also have most of these aquatic biomes located inside any of the terrestrial or climate-based biomes, with the exception of coral reefs, which are sensitive to temperature.

To give you a starting point in visualising this information, here's a map of the key biomes as we find them on Earth.

PART ONE: THE BIOMES

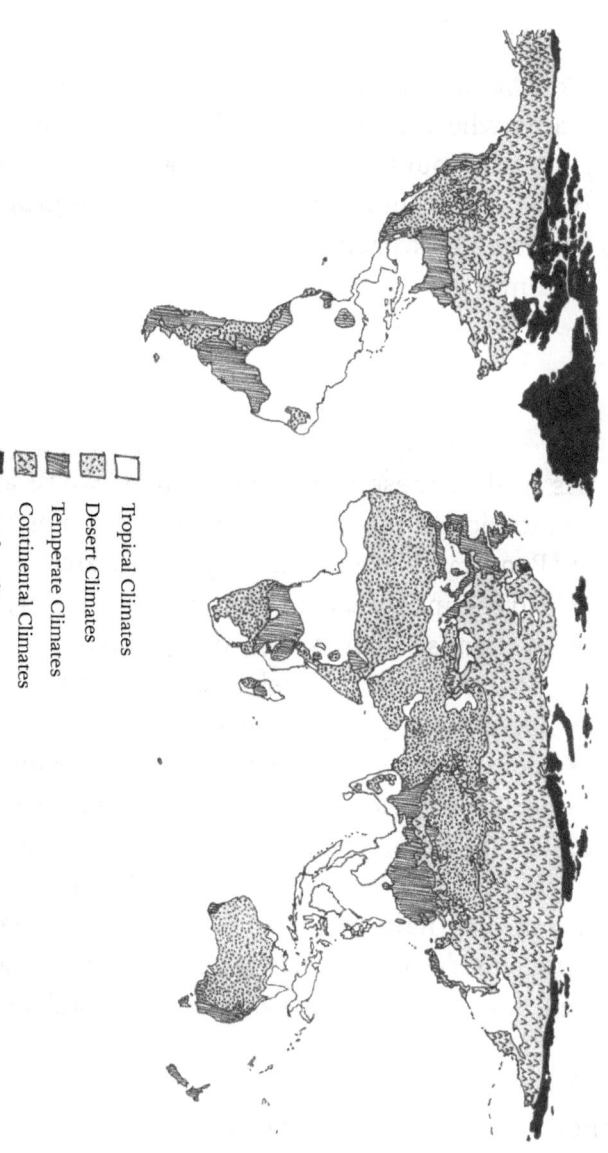

PART ONE: THE BIOMES

For each of these biomes, we will explore the general characteristics of each before turning to the characteristics of the populations. I also provide a list of common plants, foods and animals for each biome to get you started. These lists are not exhaustive, and you can use them as the basis for inventing your own plant and animal species (though for more detail on how to do that, and on how plants and animals adapt to their environment, see *How To Create Life* in the *Inkprint Writers* series).

However, remember that plants and animals *are* specific to their environments as well: just as you can't pick up one culture and plonk it down into another biome and expect it to work, you can't pick up a polar bear and drop it into the tropics, or substitute a hedgehog for a monkey just because they're both omnivores. (Unless that conflict is central to your story.)

So, the lists are not comprehensive, but they *are* a list of suggests of plants and animals that will *work* in that environment.

TROPICAL CLIMATES: RAIN FORESTS AND DRY FORESTS

Tropical climates include both rain forest biomes and dry forest biomes. Although both have distinct features in terms of climate, plant life and animal life, both are similar in terms of the types of cultures that tend to form in them.

RAIN FOREST BIOMES

In tropical rain forests, both the temperatures and humidity levels remain stable and high throughout the year, and rainfall is also high year round (although there can be a little seasonal variation). Average daytime temperatures are around 27C/80F, and humidity is usually between 77% and 88%. Because of the high surface temperature and high humidity, cumulus clouds form almost every afternoon—one source of all that rain.

Tropical rain forests have soils that are high in iron- or aluminium-oxide and are therefore reddish in colour. They are poor in organic matter and nutrients, although there is usually a thick layer of decaying organic matter over top of the soil. Because of this, vegetation tends to be shallow-rooted and to rely heavily on sunlight and rain for its nutrients. Luckily, both sunlight and rain are abundant in a tropical rain forest, meaning plants often grow huge leaves to capitalise on photosynthesis, and grow tall to compete for sunlight. In fact, rain forests arrange themselves fairly neatly into four layers:

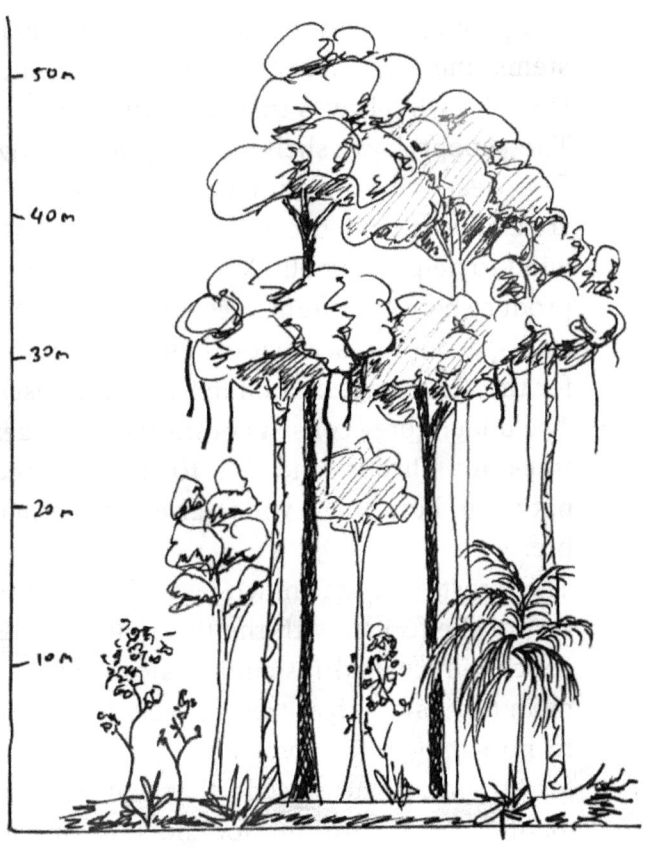

- The <u>emergent</u> layer consists of the tallest and oldest trees (the ones *emerging* out the top). These trees bear the brunt of climactic change and receive most of the sunlight. They are home to bromeliads, which are specialised plants that have developed the ability to do without roots, instead capturing and pooling moisture from the rain in their stems and leaves, and absorbing nutrients from decaying leaves that fall into them.
- The <u>canopy</u> layer shelters the layers below from heat, wind and rain. Creepers and vines are abundant, and because there is very little wind to help with pollination, plants tend to produce berries or nuts to encourage animals to disperse their seeds for them (one reason for the abundance of food in the rain forest).
- The <u>understorey</u> consists of shorter, younger trees and shrubs, and due to its sheltered nature is home to a wide variety of animal life.
- The <u>forest floor</u> gets much less rain than the rest of the forest, with the little rain it does get coming from drips and trickles down the main trunks of larger trees. It also gets little to no sunlight. To combat this, many rain-forest species have seeds that can lie dormant for years, waiting for the sunshine to appear when a larger tree falls. When this

happens, a race between seedlings begins as they compete for resources. There also isn't as much animal life on the floor of the forest, as it's harder to defend yourself there than in the understorey.

Overall, tropical rain forests harbour the largest biodiversity (range of species) of all the biomes. The exact reason for this is still unknown, but it's likely because the climate in tropical rain forest areas remains stable throughout the year; it's much easier to exist in a stable environment than it is to live in one where the temperatures or rainfall change seasonally and require you to be prepared for extremes.

KEY RAIN FOREST PLANTS

Vegetation is characterised by:
- Broad-leafed, evergreen trees
- Ferns or palms
- Large, woody vines and climbing plants
- Orchids
- Bromeliads

Fruits include:
- Persimmons
- Avocados
- Bananas

TROPICAL FORESTS

- Betel nuts
- Coconuts
- Custard apples
- Some hot-climate cherries
- Gooseberries
- Dragonfruit
- Guava
- Grapes
- Grapefruit
- Rambutans
- Almonds
- Jackfruit
- Lychees
- Lemons
- Mangoes
- Tamarinds
- Macadamias
- Olives
- Oranges
- Nutmeg
- Allspice
- Pineapples
- Pistachios
- Pecans
- Passionfruit
- Papaya
- Pomegranates
- Tangerines
- Watermelons

TROPICAL FORESTS

- Other fruits, nuts and spices that are intolerant to frost

KEY RAIN FOREST ANIMALS

- Hundreds of thousands of insects and arachnids of all varieties, including huge tarantula spiders;
- Vast numbers of bird species, including parrots, parakeets, toucans, macaws, cockatoos, finches, cockatiels, kingfishers, cassowaries, hornbills, owls and more;
- Reptiles including a significant array of lizards, most of the world's frog species, snakes of many kinds, caiman and turtles;
- Herbivores including sloths, tapirs, capybaras, herbivorous monkeys and in large rain forest rivers, manatees or dugongs;
- Omnivores such as omnivorous monkeys, including tamarins;
- Carnivores or insectivores such as bats, piranha, anteaters, cats like ocelots and jaguars, and even dolphins.

DRY FOREST BIOMES

Tropical dry forests have high average temperatures all year round and very high levels of rainfall, but unlike tropical rain forests, they have a distinct dry season. Because of this, plants and animals all have features that allow them to survive extended periods without access to water.

For plants, this mostly means that they are deciduous. Most plants in a tropical dry forest will shed their leaves during the dry season, enabling them to conserve precious water that would otherwise be lost through their leaves during the day.

Some plants have green trunks so that they can still photosynthesise even without leaves; some store water in swollen roots or trunks for use during dry periods so they don't have to shed their leaves.

Plants that don't drop their leaves in the dry season usually have waxy leaves that don't lose water easily (for example many species of eucalypt), and some even fold their leaves closed together at night ('nyctinasty') to prevent further water loss (for example the twisted acacia, scientific name *vachellia tortuosa*).

Dry forest animals have also developed behaviours that enable them to survive dry periods. Many frogs and insects enter estivation—the summer equivalent of hibernation. They retreat to burrows, or simply dig themselves deep down into the mud, and wait for the water to return. Larger animals, such as birds and monkeys, congregate around streambeds, demonstrating a tolerance for crowds that they would never accept in the wet season.

During the dry season, the forests are comparatively still. However, at the first rains, the forest explodes into life. New leaves grow rapidly and plants fruit, providing food for hungry critters that quickly set about finding mates and reproducing. At the peak of the wet season, the forest is teeming with life, and as the rains draw to their end, plants burst into frenzied bloom in an attempt to attract pollinators before the dry period arrives. These pollinated seeds lie dormant for the dry season, ready to sprout as soon as the rains arrive once more.

KEY DRY FOREST PLANTS

Vegetation includes:
- Orchids
- Bromeliads
- Palms
- Teak
- Ash species
- Acacias (including wattles)
- Eucalypts

Fruits include:
- Figs
- Grapes

TROPICAL FORESTS

- Pomegranates
- Blood oranges and oranges
- Limes including key, kaffir, Persian and the Australian finger lime
- Mandarins
- Tangerines
- Kumquats
- Lemons and sweet lemons
- Avocados
- Lychees
- Carob
- Feijoas
- Guava
- Longans
- Passionfruit
- Peanuts
- Dates
- Tamarillos

KEY DRY FOREST ANIMALS

Although tropical dry forests are not as diverse as tropical wet forests, they still host an extremely large number of species, particularly insects and birds. Wildlife includes:

- Insects and arachnids such as ants (carpenter ants, army ants, acacia ants, etc.), scorpions, bees, moths, stick insects, termites, and many, many more (including puppy-sized spiders!);

- Birds such as woodpeckers, parakeets, doves, owls, hawks, hummingbirds, kites, harriers, pelicans, hornbills and more;
- A huge range of frogs and toads;
- Snakes and lizards in abundance, as these tough-skinned creatures are well-suited to dry periods;
- Herbivores such as tapir, Howler and other monkeys, peccaries, elephants, rhinoceroses, giraffes, various deer species, and rodents: agoutis, squirrels, rats and mice, etc.;
- Omnivores such as foxes, hedgehogs, coati and various types of bears;
- Insectivores such as anteaters;
- Carnivores such as ocelots, tigers, cougars, lynx, bobcats, jaguars and wolves.

As is apparent from this list, there are a lot more mammals in a tropical dry forest than in a tropical wet forest, even though tropical wet forests have greater overall biodiversity due to their stable climates.

FOOD IN TROPICAL (RAIN AND DRY FOREST) CLIMATES

In comparison to temperate biomes, the soil in tropical rain forests is less rich in nutrients. This means it's harder to grow food than in temperate regions, so populations tend to be smaller and less dense.

Food in tropical climates goes off extremely quickly; for populations without access to refrigeration this means frequent harvesting or trips to markets for fresh goods, rather than large-scale shopping or gathering trips.

This, plus a climate that allows a wide range of plants to grow very quickly, means that diets largely consist of a variety of freshly-prepared fruits and vegetables, with meat as a supplement for those who can afford it.

Due to the high temperatures year round, cooking is often done quickly and simply, with stir-frying a popular method. Many strong spices (for example ginger, chilli, turmeric and curry) thrive best in tropical environments; strongly spiced food also provokes a cooling reaction in the body. (Have you ever sweated while eating a really strong curry? That's this reaction at work!) Because of this, many tropical cuisines feature strong spices.

As well as the various fruits listed above (not an exhaustive list), palms thrive throughout tropical regions, and the sap of many species of palm tree is edible, and can be used to make palm wines.

TROPICAL FORESTS

CLOTHING IN TROPICAL (RAIN AND DRY FOREST) CLIMATES

The emphasis in tropical areas is on lightweight, breathable clothing, for obvious reasons! Breathability is especially important in tropical climates not just for comfort, but also because the humidity causes people to sweat heavily, which can lead easily to skin infections if hygiene is poor, or if clothing seals sweat and its accompanying bacteria against the skin.

Fabric made from natural fibres breathes more effectively than synthetic fibres; thus hemp, silk, linen and cotton are the preferred fabrics, depending on what's available in the area. Likewise, clothing styles that allow airflow, but that also don't flap about and impede movement, are preferred.

SHELTER AND THE ENVIRONMENT IN TROPICAL (RAIN AND DRY FOREST) CLIMATES

Wood is plentiful in the tropical environment, but the constant dampness of the climate, both from rainfall and humidity, mean that it needs to be replaced on a fairly regular basis, as it's prone to rot. The humidity and consistently high temperatures of the climate mean that housing must be designed to maximise airflow and shade. Houses may sometimes be built on stilts to avoid flooding and increase airflow around the building.

Palm leaves of various types are often used for roofing as, if tightly woven, they can be extremely waterproof while still allowing ventilation both for air and smoke from cooking fires. High ceilings can also assist in keeping living areas cooler, as can designs that maximise external wall area—long, thin buildings are much more effective for staying cool than square-shaped buildings. Raised sleep areas can also be a cooling design feature.

MARRIAGE AND THE FAMILY IN TROPICAL (RAIN AND DRY FOREST) CLIMATES

While there are no generalisations that can be drawn regarding marriage in tropical climates simply because there is too great a variety of options, in many tropical cultures there are no marriage rituals, or only very limited ones. Again, while it's inaccurate to generalise across all tropical populations, there are many tropical populations wherein marriage is simply formalised by the birth of the first child. Alternatively, marriages may be conducted all together in a mass ceremony during the dry season.

There are, of course, numerous examples of other options, but these are two that are reasonably common.

Children are often carried with the mother while they are unable to walk steadily and independently, as the forest floors can be uneven and full of trip hazards. This means there is a slight tendency for children to be spaced about two and a half to three years apart, as by this time the child is weaned and able to follow along independently without too much trouble. Also, by this age children can more easily be left in the care of older children.

ECONOMIC DEVELOPMENT IN TROPICAL (RAIN AND DRY FOREST) CLIMATES

Tropical rainforests are often dense and difficult to travel through, making the transport of goods very difficult. Because of this, in a true rainforest the populations are likely to be small and self-sufficient. However, the fringes of the rainforests provide a hospitable environment for daily life and a convenient location for economic development; in these fringe areas products like cotton, crude oil, cocoa, coffee, and other tropical crops can be important sources of income.

Palms, too, provide many varied products, such as food (coconuts, wines from the various saps, edible oils), building materials, fuel, agricultural implements, clothing, furniture, jewellery, material for various household items such as bowls and mats, stationery to write on, musical instruments, flowers for ornamental and ritual use, saps and other plant matter for medicines, and more.

Metals, on the other hand, are often difficult to come by in tropical areas and so must usually be imported, although the high incidence of oxisol soils in rainforests can provide iron and aluminium ores if the culture has the technological means to mine them.

HEALTH AND MEDICINE IN TROPICAL (RAIN AND DRY FOREST) CLIMATES

Due to the hot, humid conditions in the tropical climate, fungal infections are common. Likewise, infections of minor injuries can be common compared to other climates, as bacteria thrive in the warm, moist environment. Parasites are also common in tropical areas for the same reason.

Insect-borne diseases pose a serious threat, particularly in the case of dangerous conditions such as malaria. Insects thrive in the tropics, breeding and multiplying far better than the proverbial rabbits, so precautions like insect nets can be common.

As well as spreading disease, insects and insect-like creatures can cause trouble with their own bites, especially arachnids such as ticks and spiders.

Snakebites and general animal attacks are also common concerns in tropical areas, simply because there's so much wildlife around.

In low-tech societies, medical treatments tend to be based on the locally available plant life (as in all climates), as well as the more poisonous and/or venomous species of insects and animals, snakes being a favourite.

ART AND LEISURE IN TROPICAL (RAIN AND DRY FOREST) CLIMATES

Weaving and wood working straddle the boundary between luxury and necessity in tropical climates (and, indeed, in many others); on the one hand, both skills are vital for the successful development of a tropical population, but on the other hand, since they are so commonly used, truly skilled practitioners can elevate them to an art form.

In many cultures throughout the world, weaving is a traditionally female art, while woodworking is traditionally male.

TROPICAL SAVANNAHS

Tropical savannahs are hot year-round but have a long dry season during their summer, followed by a shorter wet season. This means that they receive more rain than deserts in similar locations, but less than tropical dry forests. Because of this lesser rainfall, there aren't as many trees in a savannah. Instead, the landscape is dominated by grasses of various kinds that can sometimes grow taller than a person, punctuated by single trees or small groves, and sometimes small shrubs. These trees and shrubs are drought-tolerant and hardy:

- They have long, deep taproots to reach the deep water table;
- They have smaller, tougher leaves that are often waxy;
- As in a tropical dry forest, their leaves may close up at night, or the tree may be deciduous;
- They may store water in their trunks or roots
- Many have thick, tough bark that helps them to survive the inevitable fires that occur in the hot, dry season;
- Some trees and shrubs even have seeds that will not germinate unless they have been through a fire.

TROPICAL SAVANNAHS

Another factor that prevents trees from taking hold is the soil situation in a savannah. Savannah soils are often (though not always) sandy and low in fertility, and they get waterlogged during the rainy season—they might even be covered in standing water for the whole length of the season.

As always, the soil characteristics are also affected by other features of the biome: soils in African savannahs are often highly compacted because of the large numbers of hoofed mammals that live there. Australian savannahs, by contrast, have older but much softer, less compacted soils, even though they have a similar climate. This is because there are no native hoofed animals: instead of hooves, Australian savannah mammals all have soft feet (like kangaroos).

Grasses are a different story. Grasses are one of the most plentiful plant families on the planet, covering about 20% of its surface, and most grass species grow from the bottom up (rather than producing new leaves at the tips of branches like trees do), so the tip of each blade is the oldest part of the plant. This protects them from damage by grazers (and lawnmowers!), allowing them to be eaten down to the ground without dying off, and also insulating them from the effects of fire.

Many grasses also have other features that protect them from being over-eaten, the most common being a bitter or unpalatable taste. In savannahs, where there can be hundreds of grass species that all taste quite different, this actually supports a greater diversity of animals. If there are a hundred species of grass that all taste very different, and each animal species eats only a particular kind of grass, a hundred different species can flourish without ever competing for food—which is exactly what happens.

Another fun trick grasses can play on their devourers is messing around with their hormones. Clovers in particular produce a hormone that mimics the action of estrogens in the mammalian body. The more endangered the plant 'feels', the more of the hormone it will produce.

You might wonder why a plant that felt endangered would be compelled to produce estrogens—unless of course you knew that estradiol, a particular type of estrogen, is the active hormone in the contraceptive pill, which in large enough doses can prevent a woman from becoming pregnant.

Sheer genius: the plant senses that it is being eaten away at a rate that will kill it off, and so increases its production of a hormone that will decrease the fertility of the animals eating it. Fewer babies, fewer grass-predators, and the grass can grow back to full strength and vibrancy. (This is also beneficial for the grazers themselves, as it helps provide a natural barrier to overpopulation.)

TROPICAL SAVANNAHS

Many animals on the savannah have long, strong legs or, in the case of birds, wings, which allow them to migrate seasonally in search of food. This migration is vital in maintaining the health of the savannah; if the herds were to stay in one location, the available vegetation would soon be eaten up, and the area would turn into a desert.

Smaller animals may create burrows or dens to avoid the summer heat, and since sweating would waste precious water, most animals will pant to cool down, or will lose heat through large areas of exposed skin (such as elephants' ears) instead. In the Australian savannahs, kangaroos lick themselves in order to increase evaporative cooling over their skin and fur.

KEY TROPICAL SAVANNAH PLANTS

Common plants differ according to location, and in fact many savannahs can be further classified by the dominant species of tree: acacia savannahs, pine savannahs, palm savannahs and eucalypt savannahs.

African-style savannahs may also have:
- Baobabs
- Elephant grass
- Manketti and Jackal berry trees
- Candelabra trees
- Bermuda grass, etc.

TROPICAL SAVANNAHS

Australian-style savannahs have mostly:
- Eucalypts such as the Jarrah
- Other shorter grasses
- Other drought-hardy plants such as the kangaroo paw, etc.

Few fruits are native to the savannah climate due to the extensive dry period.

KEY TROPICAL SAVANNAH ANIMALS

Due to the abundance of grasses, the largest savannahs in the world are home to a high concentration of herding, herbivorous mammals in a wide variety of sizes and heights.

Antelopes particularly are abundant, with elands, impalas, gazelles, oryx, and more.

Other African herbivores include:
- Buffalo
- Wildebeest
- Zebras
- Giraffes
- Elephants
- Rhinoceroses
- Warthogs

In areas with enough water, you might also find hippopotamuses.

This huge array of herbivores in turn supports a large range of carnivores, including:

- Members from the feline family (lions, leopards, cheetahs, servals);
- Member from the canine family (jackals, wild dogs, dingos);
- Others such as crocodiles (particularly saltwater species), hyenas, and mongooses.

Abundant termites and ants in all types of savannahs provide food for:
- Anteaters
- Pangolins
- Aardvarks
- Echidnas

Additionally, there are:
- Reptiles of all kinds, particularly snakes and lizards
- Baboons in some cases (the most notable of the omnivores)
- Plentiful bird species, including many hawks and eagles (which find the grasslands an ideal hunting ground), ostriches or emus, weaverbirds, storks and more.

In the Australian savannahs, the non-bird wildlife generally reflects the rest of the Australian continent:
- Approximately one third bats (usually insectivores);

TROPICAL SAVANNAHS

- One fifth rodents (usually rabbit-sized or smaller, and frequently nocturnal);
- A few reptiles (snakes and lizards, mostly);
- And the remainder are marsupials such as kangaroos, wallabies, bandicoots, dunnarts, possums, and quolls.

Also found in Australian savannahs are birds such as:
- Emus
- Wrens
- Bee-eaters
- Honey-eaters
- Shrike-thrushes
- Butcherbirds
- Black cockatoos

FOOD IN TROPICAL SAVANNAHS

Given the prevalence of grasses and the comparative scarcity of trees, it's not surprising that grains and legumes form the basis of many tropical savannah diets. Indeed, sub-Saharan Africa boasts a wider variety of native grains than anywhere else in the world.

As in other tropical climates, plant matter forms the majority of the diet, with meat used as supplementary flavouring rather than as a main feature.

TROPICAL SAVANNAHS

Stews are extremely common, with flavours characteristic of the plants (particularly herbs and spices) native to the area. These stews are often served over a root vegetable mash (cassava grows well in tropical savannahs, though it is toxic unless thoroughly cooked) or a grain porridge.

Flavours are also influenced by trade routes. Places in Africa that formed part of the key supply route during the reign of the British Empire formed connections to India that heavily influenced their cuisine, and as a result, many traditionally Indian spices have become integral to their cooking.

CLOTHING IN TROPICAL SAVANNAHS

Australia and Africa boast the highest diversity of native cotton species in the world (along with Mexico), and the majority of these species are found in the tropical savannahs. Accordingly, much of the clothing that appears in tropical savannahs is based on cotton cloth, often woven into wide bolts or square cloths that are tied or draped or wrapped around the body.

Animal hides can also be used for clothing, as mammals with appropriate skins are very common in this climate (including various varieties of cows, sheep, goats, elephants and marsupial possums), and hair or wool from grazing animals is also available.

Alternatively, given the warmth of the climate, some populations may shun clothing altogether; there are many tribes from the Australian savannahs who wore only body paint, with maybe something protective over the genitals for men.

Finally, bark-cloth might also be used to fashion clothing, made by stripping stringy bark from certain types of trees and using the fibres to create first thread, then cloth. Raffia, spinifex, or other strong plant fibres can also be used in the same way.

SHELTER AND THE ENVIRONMENT IN TROPICAL SAVANNAHS

Due to the comparative lack of trees and therefore wood, many permanent structures in the savannah are made from a wattle-and-daub construction. This is where a woven frame is constructed from lightweight wood or strong grasses, and then sealed with packing material—usually a mixture of wet soil, clay, straw and animal dung.

Grasses and straws are often used for the roof material. Populations in the savannah can also be nomadic, following the natural migration of the many large herds of grazing animals. In this case, skins might be used to construct portable tents.

TROPICAL SAVANNAHS

As in other tropical climates, air circulation is a high priority to facilitate cooling. Because of this, houses that maximise external wall area and minimise internal walls can be preferred. This can mean long, skinny buildings, or a series of interconnected huts each devoted to a specific purpose, as rooms under the one roof would be.

Basic huts might also be constructed over platforms, under which a fire would be kept burning overnight so that the smoke would drive away mosquitos.

ECONOMIC DEVELOPMENT IN TROPICAL SAVANNAHS

Although parts of the savannah that experience comparatively less rainfall might not be able to support crops, in general the savannah supports a wide variety of agriculture. Grains in particular are abundant.

Yams, oil palms, raffia palms, millet, watermelons, gourds, coffee and cotton are just some of the crops that were domesticated in savannah regions before being exported to the rest of the world.

Sugar, coffee, tobacco and tea also grow well in the savannah environment.

Additionally, bauxite (for aluminium), copper, gold, iron ore, platinum, chrome and uranium are just some of the many valuable minerals that are commonly found in the soil of tropical savannahs.

Populations in these regions can also be nomadic and can either rely on hunting (denoting a primarily hunter-gatherer economy) or on herding (implying a more agricultural-based economy, likely based on exchange, whether of goods or of currency). Cows, sheep and particularly goats are all important domestic animals in this climate.

HEALTH AND MEDICINE IN TROPICAL SAVANNAHS

Tuberculosis, malaria and HIV/AIDS are some of the major causes of death in savannah areas today. Interestingly, these three conditions are all thought to be native to the savannah biome.

The HIV virus is thought to have originated in tropical Africa, first in chimpanzees, transferring to humans when chimpanzee meat was consumed.

Tuberculosis is also believed to have originated in the African savannahs, around about the same time the very first villages were constructed.

Likewise, malaria is believed to have co-evolved alongside the very first human populations and is facilitated by mosquitos, which thrive in all tropical biomes, especially during wet seasons.

Helpfully, the key ingredient in treating malaria—quinine—is also native to the African tropical savannah, found in the bark of the cinchona tree.

ART AND LEISURE IN TROPICAL SAVANNAHS

While artwork throughout the savannah regions of the world is obviously very diverse, there are nonetheless a few key themes. Human figures are the most common subjects, and art is often created with the dual purpose of being beautiful and also practical. There is often little distinction between an artist, who creates something of beauty to be admired, and a craftsman, who creates tools and other objects for ordinary use with extreme skill.

Sculpture is another common theme, as are other kinds of three-dimensional or performative art: wood carvings, beadwork and jewellery, music, and dance all feature heavily. Symbolic use of size—exaggerating the most important features, for example—is also common.

DESERTS

Deserts are characterised first and foremost by their lack of rainfall. They include both semi-arid areas and true deserts. Because of the lack of rainfall and groundwater that would usually transport minerals and clay particles down and away through the ground, desert soils are often mineral-rich and sandy, with true soil taking a long time to form.

Another characteristic of desert areas is the wide contrast between day and night time temperatures; because there is little of both water and vegetation to act as insulation, and because rock both absorbs heat quickly and loses it quickly, temperatures soar during the day time and plummet at night. This means that any plant and animal life must be able to exist with very little water and also be able to withstand extremes of hot and cold.

Beyond this, however, deserts can vary widely in their ability to support life, depending on their latitude, altitude and the amount of wind.

Actually, wind is the major factor influencing the formation of sand dunes in deserts. Large, rolling sand dunes are often the first image that comes to mind when people mention deserts, but these dunes can only form when the prevailing winds first cross areas of exposed sand (or sandy soil) and are then interrupted by an obstacle that make them drop their load. This obstacle can be as simple as a shrub, or even a depression in the ground; if the wind is carrying a lot of sand, even something small can be enough for the wind to slow slightly or change course and drop some of its load.

Over time, the dropped sand builds in a heap, climbing steadily until the angle of it becomes sharp enough that the wind can't simply sweep back down the other side. This leads to a dune, with a smooth, gradually-climbing windward side, and a rougher, often steeper, leeward side where sand slips down from the dune's peak.

These dunes then become barriers encouraging the wind to drop even more sand in this area, and gradually this can lead to the 'desertification' of an area.

Interestingly, the slippage of sand from dunes can result in some unusual noises. Many of us may have experienced 'squeaky' sand on a beach—clean, fine, dry and often white sand that squeaks as we walk in it. This squeaky beach sand can extend inland for about 30 metres, and sand slipping down the leeward side of coastal dunes can produce this same squeak. (It's not entirely clear exactly what causes some sands to squeak, but it is known that they must have been recently 'washed' by water in some way and then dried.)

DESERTS

In contrast, inland sand that has been dry for several weeks can give off a deep, loud booming noise as it slips. This booming has been described as humming, moaning, drumming, thundering, or even likened to the drone of low-flying aircraft. Again, it's not clear what causes sand to boom, but it is a unique and intriguing feature of desert dunes.

KEY DESERT PLANTS

The majority of plants in the desert environment are succulents of one type or another, of which cacti are a major subgroup. Succulents are characterised by fleshy or swollen leaves (or sometimes stems) that act as reservoirs of moisture for the plant. Visually, succulents can range from short ground covers with tiny, bead-like leaves, all the way up to great trees with bulbous trunks, and every size in between.

Commonly known varieties include:
- Aloes and agaves
- Prickly pears
- Barrel cacti
- Saguaro
- Crimson hedgehogs

Also commonly found in deserts are:
- Joshua trees

- Creosote bushes
- Brittle bushes
- Baobab trees
- A variety of desert grasses

KEY DESERT ANIMALS

Because they are more drought tolerant, insects, arachnids and reptiles dominate the desert landscape, including:
- Ants
- Beetles
- Flies
- Wasps
- Scorpions
- Tortoises
- Snakes, including rattlesnakes
- A huge array of lizards

However, desert mammals do certainly exist:
- Most common are small-framed rodents;
- Some larger herbivorous mammals such as mule deer, antelopes and desert bighorn sheep are found;
- And there are carnivores such as mountain lions, grey foxes, and bobcats, etc.

These animals generally survive the harsh desert climate by limiting their activity either solely to the night time (nocturnal) or to dawn and dusk (crepuscular).

DESERTS

Birds also make their homes in desert environments: hawks, eagles and owls are common, as the treeless, open spaces make an ideal hunting ground for them.

FOOD IN DESERTS

While the stereotypical image of a desert is of vast, rolling dunes of nothing but sand as far as the eye can see, in fact this only applies to a minority of deserts. Most deserts can support sporadic vegetation and, in turn, some animal life. Many deserts—the type most commonly inhabited by human populations—are even capable of supporting small herds of larger mammals such as camels and goats. These can be herded for milk and also for meat. Lizards and insects also make good sources of protein.

Cacti are common in deserts, and most of them bear edible fruits. Their inner pulp is also often edible, though it usually provides a source of liquid rather than a source of calories.

Oases are another important source of food; date palms, pistachios and almonds all do well in desert cli-mates, and pecan trees will also survive, although they will not produce large crops.

Some acacia species also produce edible seeds and shoots, and some grain-bearing plants grow in desert climates, particularly desert amaranth.

DESERTS

However, due to the general lack of vegetation in deserts, diets trend towards meat rather than plant matter, with flesh and dairy products making up the bulk of the calories and plant matter forming a supplement.

CLOTHING IN DESERTS

Optimal desert clothing is loose and flowing to allow for maximum airflow, and hence evaporative cooling over the skin. Clothing that covers the entire body is preferable, as it provides protection from direct sunlight and from wind, which can dry the skin out immensely. Full coverings can also protect against painful rashes and grazes that would otherwise be caused by sand particles blowing against the body.

Interestingly enough, colour doesn't seem to make much of a difference; although black cloth absorbs more heat initially than white, so long as the garment is loose, this extra heat is all lost before it can reach the skin and heat up the person. And in actual fact, white-haired or white-feathered creatures get more heat on their skins than black-haired or -feathered creatures.

Plant matter is obviously scarce, so most cloth tends to be woven from wool (from goats, sheep, camels, or something else, depending on what the population has access to) or is traded for. Wool is a good choice, though, because it is a superior insulator, keeping the wearing warm when the weather is cold (by trapping body heat in) and cool when the weather is hot (by keeping environmental heat out).

Additionally, wool is colourfast once it has been dyed; is resistant to fire, mildew, and water; is hypoallergenic; wicks moisture away from the skin; and continues to insulate even when wet. Wool doesn't need to be washed as often as other fabrics either, as it's stain resistant and has antimicrobial properties which mean it doesn't hold smells or harbour bacteria. This also helps reduce body odours.

SHELTER AND THE ENVIRONMENT IN DESERTS

The vast majority of desert populations are nomadic or semi-nomadic, following food and

DID YOU KNOW?

In some populations, clothing can be personally significant, as the individual may not own many other possessions that are exclusively theirs. Some desert populations have developed traditions whereby a person's clothing is left on top of their grave. Often, travellers are welcome to claim this clothing.

water sources as they are able, making tents the most common form of shelter. These are often made from hides or felted fibres, or in less arid areas, branches and plant matter.

Tents might be separated by screens or cloths to create rooms, which in many areas are used to segregate genders.

Beasts of burden are also common, as it's simply too hot to carry goods oneself. Indeed, heavier items might be cached, either in caves, hidden in rock formations, or simply buried, instead of attempting to transport them at all.

MARRIAGE AND THE FAMILY IN DESERTS

Because food in the desert is such a precious resource, populations—especially of the nomadic or semi-nomadic variety—are severely constrained in size. Nomadic populations that rely on hunting and gathering for food might not be able to support more than fifteen or twenty individuals together, fragmenting and splitting relatively frequently as children are born, grow up, and form families of their own. In some cases, this might even vary seasonally, with semi-permanent dwellings occupied in winter, and a more nomadic lifestyle followed in summer—sometimes in units as small as just the nuclear family.

Marriages are likely to be arranged, as meeting in social situations is rather unlikely. Hospitality, however, is likely to be emphasised, as being able to 'drop in' on another family—particularly in the case of nomadic herders—may mean the difference between life and death in the harsh desert climate.

ECONOMIC DEVELOPMENT IN DESERTS

Many deserts were once shallow seas, and with surprising frequency overlie significant deposits of oil and natural gas. For cultures that have the technology to extract these materials, they can form the backbone of the desert's economy—as can solar energy.

Deserts generally are also mineral rich, containing—depending on their precise chemical makeup and geological history—gypsum, sodium nitrate (for fertiliser and explosives), borax, iron, sodium chloride (table salt) and uranium, amongst other compounds.

Some deserts can also be repurposed for agriculture if enough water can be diverted from nearby rivers; the soils tend to be sufficiently nutrient-rich to support a wide variety of crops.

While many desert cultures have been based on hunter-gatherer economies, many have also relied on trade. Deserts often lie in the way of major supply lines and must either be crossed by the populations on either side, or else arrangements must be made to trade with the populations that live nomadically in the desert.

These nomadic tribes might also keep herds, moving around to follow the sporadic rainfall; cattle, sheep, goats, camels, yaks and llamas are popular options, providing milk, meat and hides. Trading posts and accommodation might spring up as more permanent settlements around oases, especially if these oases correspond with key trade routes.

HEALTH AND MEDICINE IN DESERTS

Obviously, heat is a major source of health problems for people in desert climates if they are not experienced in managing it. Heatstroke, sunburn, and various eye problems can all-too-easily occur if adequate shade isn't found during the heat of the day.

Dehydration is another obvious concern, and food poisoning can occur if food is left out in the heat for too long.

Respiratory problems are also common in desert climates due to the exceptionally dry air and wide variation between day and night time temperatures. These factors exacerbate conditions such as asthma, and pulmonary tuberculosis is also common.

Most permanent residents of desert regions will have some degree of dust build-up in their lungs; often this isn't an issue, but sometimes it can result in silicosis, a condition with similar symptoms to pulmonary oedema (fluid in the lungs): shortness of breath, cough, fever and cyanosis (or blue-tinted skin, caused by insufficient oxygen supply).

Fungal diseases (such as desert fever) can also be an issue in some areas, as various fungi progress through most of their life cycle very quickly when it rains, releasing potentially millions of spores that then settle into the desert dust to await the next rainfall. These spores can be stirred up by any disturbance of the dirt, and if inhaled can cause a variety of complications, depending on the species of fungus.

Scorpions, spiders and snakes are also comparatively abundant, though their bites or stings are rarely fatal.

Finally, desert storms, including sand storms, lightning storms, and tornadoes, can also pose a significant risk to human populations, requiring them to seek shelter until the storms pass.

DESERTS

ART AND LEISURE IN DESERTS

Dance is an important means of expression for many desert cultures, often linked tightly with religious beliefs, and, as in many cultures, music is also integral to society.

Weaving and beading are relatively common forms of art, while pottery and sculpture much rarer due to their excessive weight. Drawing and painting are relatively common too, with some of the oldest rock paintings in the world originating from desert cultures.

The invention of calligraphy is also credited to desert cultures, originally for religious reasons (because creating sculptures or images of a deity could be considered idolatry).

Team sports or games, on the other hand, are slightly less common in desert climates than elsewhere, and individual tests of strength or endurance slightly more common.

TEMPERATE CLIMATES: GRASSLANDS, WOODLANDS AND FORESTS

Temperate climates include grasslands, woodlands and forests. Although each of these have distinct features in terms of climate, plant life and animal life, they're similar in terms of the types of cultures that tend to form in them.

TEMPERATE GRASSLAND BIOMES

Temperate grasslands, which include prairies and steppes, generally have warm, moist summers and cool, dry winters. They receive a moderate amount of rain year-round, though less than tropical savannahs, and have fertile soils. They are characterised by lush, perennial grasses and herbs, and are found on all continents on Earth except Africa. As with savannahs, fires are commonplace in grasslands and much of the plant life is resistant to them, as well as extremes of hot and cold (see the section on savannahs for more information on grasses in particular).

Trees don't grow in temperate grasslands; there isn't enough consistent rainfall throughout the year—and in grasslands with higher latitudes (i.e. closer to the poles), much of the rain may fall as snow during winter, only melting to provide water for plants in the spring. Grazing by large herbivores also prevents tree growth, although a few species (cottonwoods, oaks, willows and other similar trees) can grow along riverbeds.

Grasses are ideally suited to this climate, forming dense root networks that make them able to withstand long periods without much moisture. These root networks also serve to keep the soil in place, and grass blades that die off and rot away contribute to the high percentage of organic matter in the rich, black, fertile soil. However, these roots also prevent tree growth, as they can choke potential seedlings before they establish themselves.

Temperate grasslands have natural appeal for human populations as they provide land that is ideal for agriculture: flat, treeless expanses with very rich soil. However, over-tilling has led to the disappearance of many of the world's temperate grasslands, particularly in the USA where prairies once dominated the Midwest. This is because agricultural tilling disrupts the extensive root networks of grasses, leading to soil erosion and degradation. As a result, immense dust storms can form when wind picks up soil from areas that were once grasslands.

TEMPERATE CLIMATES

KEY TEMPERATE GRASSLAND PLANTS

As evident from their name, grasslands are dominated by various grass species, including:
- Purple needlegrass
- Blue grama
- Buffalo grass
- Galleta
- And hundreds of others.

Small shrubs can also take hold, including:
- Asters
- Blazing stars
- Coneflowers
- Goldenrods
- Sunflowers
- Clovers
- Wild indigos, etc.

In steppe areas, cacti, sagebrush and speargrass are also found.

Trees such as cottonwoods, oaks and willows can grow along streambeds.

KEY TEMPERATE GRASSLAND ANIMALS

Wildlife diversity is not as great as in tropical or savannah areas. It includes:
- Insects and arachnids, such as spiders, ants

and grasshoppers;
- Reptiles such as snakes (including garter, brown, black and rattlesnakes) and lizards (including whiptails, earless dragons and legless lizards);
- Birds such as owls and hawks that find the open grasslands easy hunting;
- Ground-nesting or low-nesting bird species such as blackbirds, grouse, meadowlarks, quails and sparrows;
- Herbivores such as rabbits, mule deer, pronghorn antelopes, tarpan and wild horses, bison, and various rodents like groundhogs, pocket gophers, mole rats and prairie dogs;
- Small carnivores such as skunks, badgers, various members of the weasel family like black-footed ferrets, wolves;
- Omnivores like the coyote.

TEMPERATE WOODLAND BIOMES

Woodland biomes have a semi-arid climate. Their rainfall occurs mostly in winter and although the area is semi-arid, there is enough rainfall to support some trees. These trees are either deciduous, to help with water retention, or have leaves that are waxy, small, or both, to help minimise evaporation. Because summers are dry

TEMPERATE CLIMATES

and warm-to-hot, fires can occur regularly. Because of this, some plants are fire resistant, or have fire-adapted seeds that require the heat of wildfires in order to germinate.

However, waxy-leaved trees and plants often have high concentrations of flammable oils in their leaves and bark that can fuel these fires (pines, eucalypts, etc.).

Temperate woodland areas are characterised by open woodland or scrubland. In wetter temperate woodlands (verging towards the temperate forest biome), they may have four distinct storeys: the canopy of tall trees, the understorey of moderate-sized trees and large shrubs, the field layer of shorter shrubs, and the ground level grasses, lichens, and so forth. In drier temperate woodlands, there may be only a canopy and a ground level, or an understorey and a ground level.

Soils are often thin and nutrient-poor, distinguishing temperate woodlands from temperate forests, but many plants still thrive.

KEY TEMPERATE WOODLAND PLANTS

Common plants found in temperate woodlands include:
- Many common herbs, including sage, rosemary, thyme and oregano;

TEMPERATE CLIMATES

- A wide variety of grasses, including tussock grasses;
- Shrubs, including hawthorn, hazel and rhododendrons;
- Trees such as acacias (including wattles), eucalypts, oaks, and ash, etc.

KEY TEMPERATE WOODLAND ANIMALS

Animals generally have varied diets, making use of the wide variety of plants on offer. Creatures from most major animal families can be found in temperate woodlands. In the northern hemi-sphere, common species include:

- Coyotes
- Foxes
- Bobcats
- Lynxes
- Mountain lions
- Badgers
- Deer
- Squirrels
- Rabbits and hares
- Pine martens and other members of the weasel family

Australian woodlands are home to a wide variety of marsupials such as:

TEMPERATE CLIMATES

- Kangaroos
- Wallabies
- Wombats
- Possums

And other animals such as:

- Echidnas
- A variety of bats
- Flying foxes
- Owls
- Magpies
- Parrots (rosellas, galahs, cockatoos, etc)

Other temperate woodland species include:

- Hawks
- Quails
- Warblers
- Lizards
- Snakes
- Insects, including many butterflies
- Spiders
- A wide variety of deer and small rodents

TEMPERATE FOREST BIOMES

Temperate forests are similar to temperate woodlands, except they receive consistent rainfall all year round. There is wide variation in the average temperature and the exact amount of annual rainfall.

However, they are all characterised by rich, heavily organic soil and dense tree growth.

Some temperate forests may have cold winters that halt plant growth; in these areas, trees will generally be either deciduous, or they will be conifers (trees with needles instead of leaves, which also bear cones).

Temperate eucalypt forests also exist in Australia, where the trees are neither coniferous nor deciduous; species such as black or white peppermints, and snow, silver, blue or yellow gums are most common.

Temperate forests usually display all four layers of growth (canopy, understorey, field or shrub layer, and ground cover), with a wide variety of plants existing in each.

KEY TEMPERATE FOREST PLANTS

Because of the higher rainfall, plant life (and subsequently animal life) may be more diverse than in temperate woodlands. Species found may include:
- Oaks
- Ashes
- Birches
- Beeches
- Pines
- Various nut trees such as pecans

TEMPERATE CLIMATES

- Eucalypts such as black peppermints, white peppermints, snow gum, silver gums, blue gums and yellow gums
- Field maples
- Hawthorn
- Rhododendrons
- Tea trees
- Holly
- Ferns
- Sedges
- Grasses
- Mosses
- Lichens
- A wide variety of fungi

A large array of food can also be found in temperate forests:
- A plethora of herbs;
- Many types of mushroom;
- Many fruits such as apples, pears, cherries, apricots, peaches, nectarines, plums, grapes;
- Berries of all kinds;
- Vegetables such as broccoli, cabbages, peas, carrots, tomatoes, potatoes, beans, squashes and pumpkins;
- And much, much more.

This is a great biome for food diversity!

TEMPERATE CLIMATES

KEY TEMPERATE FOREST ANIMALS

Animals may need to compensate for cold winters and may hibernate or become dormant for periods of time.

Common species include:
- Deer
- Bears
- Bobcats
- Squirrels
- Chipmunks
- Raccoons
- Skunks
- Coyotes
- Foxes
- Weasels
- Rodents
- Birds including a variety of songbirds, turkeys, lyrebirds and eagles
- Marsupials such as sugar gliders, kangaroos, wallabies, wombats, possums, platypuses and echidnas

FOOD IN TEMPERATE CLIMATES

Generally speaking, temperate grasslands are grasslands because there is insufficient water to support trees. However, they are also the location of most of the world's mollisols, the fertile, black, humus-rich soils that all gardeners crave.

As a result, grasslands generally are able to a provide large array of food types—and indeed, many of the world's grasslands have been taken over for agricultural use.

Corn, wheat, barley, canola, oats, alfalfa, various grasses used for hay, and soybeans are just some of the most extensive crops grown in temperate grasslands—but as previously mentioned, most foods are able to grow easily in this climate.

Because of this, and the extensive array of grasses that can support large herds of herbivores,

Did You Know?

The famous 'Three Sisters' combination of maize, squash and beans arose in the temperate grasslands of North America. This combination of plants does so well because each plant provides something that the others need to survive: beans fix nitrogen into the soil, while maize is the gas-guzzler of the plant world and needs a lot of nitrogen to grow well. Beans need something to climb; maize has tall stalks that it doesn't mind donating to the cause. The squash is important because it provides a 'mulch', covering the soil to minimise wind and water erosion, and sheltering it to reduce evaporation and help retain moisture.

TEMPERATE CLIMATES

temperate grassland diets tend to be a fairly equal blend of meat and plant matter.

Temperate forests and woodlands, while not the most diverse in terms of total number of species, are certainly the most diverse with regards to species of plants that humans find useful. More humans live in temperate forests and woodlands than in any other biome, with some three-quarters of humanity currently residing at least in this climate type, if not in in actual forest biomes (due to urbanisation). Largely, this is because of the vast array of foods native to this climate.

Many cuisines in this climate rely on the concept of sauce; whereas cuisines in hotter areas tend to employ spices as the condiment of choice, temperate regions tend to use sauces and the like—mustard, mayonnaise, cream sauces, gravies and more. Because the winter in temperate regions is often cold, cuisines tend to feature 'heavier' dishes, rich in fats and starches.

Meat, though plentiful, is not as plentiful as the many fruits and vegetables supported by the climate, and, as in hotter areas, is often the most expensive part of the meal. Because of this, in areas with significant class segregation, meat may be reserved for the rich people; alternatively, meat may be eaten only infrequently, one or two, maybe three times a week as a supplement to an otherwise plant-based diet. It is worth noting that the

TEMPERATE CLIMATES

concept of a 'meat and three veggies' meal was invented in the temperate biome.

Yeast-risen bread is also another staple feature of temperate biomes, as the climate is warm enough for wild yeasts to ferment, but not so hot that these sourdough cultures will quickly turn rancid.

CLOTHING IN TEMPERATE CLIMATES

Clothing native to temperate areas can be made from a wide variety of materials, as plants for fibre grow readily in this climate (cotton, flax, hemp and so forth) and abundant furred animals allow for a range of animal hide options also.

Generally, clothing forms some variation on full-length or shorter leggings or pants, with a tunic-style garment over top. This tunic might be lengthened below the knee to become a dress for women in some areas.

These tunics can be decorated with bead-work and fringing (generally in the case of animal-hide clothing), or with embroidery (both hide and cloth garments), or with sashes and brocade-style embellishments (usually for cloth garments).

TEMPERATE CLIMATES

SHELTER AND THE ENVIRONMENT IN TEMPERATE CLIMATES

Plentiful food means that permanent settlements are not only more supportable, but much more likely. In fact, urbanisation generally seems to occur much faster in temperate climates than in other climates. In woodlands and forests, the building material for these settlements is generally native timber, which can lead to deforestation in some areas.

The clearing of trees for agriculture can also be a concern, though some cultures throughout history (such as the Japanese) have managed to find balance and avoid environmental disaster.

Settlements may be walled for protection in areas where the required building materials (wood or rock) are available.

In grasslands, many populations are nomadic and so use tents, often round (as in Native American tepees or Mongolian yurts), made from the hides of the animals they either herd or follow (horses, goats, sheep, cattle including bison, and so forth).

Housing in temperate grasslands varies widely according to the needs and technological abilities of the individual populations, since temperate regions generally are fairly hospitable, and prairies in particular can support a wide variety of lifestyles.

TEMPERATE CLIMATES

Notably, however, famous architect Frank Lloyd Wright invented a style of architecture known as Prairie architecture in the late 1800s to early 1900s, and it emphasised low-pitched rooves and overhanging eaves, with a central chimney and open floor plan, all in response to what he perceived to be the most important needs of the climate.

MARRIAGE AND THE FAMILY IN TEMPERATE CLIMATES

Unlike harsher climates where food constrains the size of a population or family unit, temperate biomes tend to be capable of supporting larger clans, tribes, villages, or populations generally.

Large groups can travel together with relative ease, following the herds of native grazing herbivores, and food is generally plentiful (though less so in winter), which makes it possible to support permanent settlements much more easily.

The plentiful food supply also means that family units can extend to include multiple generations; thus interfamilial communities can form more easily.

Interestingly, cultures in temperate woodlands and forests seem to be the first to have developed burial mounds, with this tradition evolving separately in numerous temperate forest or woodland regions around the world.

TEMPERATE CLIMATES

In temperate grasslands, there seems to be a very slight trend for women to have more social rights than their counterparts in other climatic regions, mostly with regards to things like property ownership, right of divorce, and custody issues. However, labour is still usually divided strictly between the genders.

There also may be a very slight trend towards less social pressure on women to hide their sexuality and remain virginal.

ECONOMIC DEVELOPMENT IN TEMPERATE CLIMATES

Temperate woodlands and forests often rely on lumber for their trade; they provide timber for ships, furniture, housing, firewood, paper, and any other uses nearby (or distant!) populations can conceive of.

Historically, because of their fertile soils, forests and woodlands in temperate regions have often been cleared for agriculture, which also provides an important source of income (until the long-term effects of deforestation are felt).

Horses are native to temperate grasslands, having arisen in the Eurasian steppes, and many grassland cultures (both where the horses are native and where they have been introduced) co-opt them for human purposes, riding them to hunt prey more efficiently and herding them for both milk and meat.

Given that grasslands provide the perfect grazing for many herbivores, and that grasses and similar plants such as cereal crops grow so well in grasslands, it's not surprising that agriculture is often an important part of temperate grassland economics.

Many grassland cultures have also been nomadic, following the natural migration of the largest herbivores. Largely the differences in economic structure in this climate zone are determined by technological factors (see Part Two), rather than by the climate, since temperate grasslands are generally supportive of a wide range of lifestyles.

HEALTH AND MEDICINE IN TEMPERATE CLIMATES

There are not many climate-specific health concerns that occur only in temperate biomes. Populations in these areas are afflicted by a similar range of bacterial, viral and fungal infections as other climates, and when medicating use local plants and animal life in their cures, according to the technology available.

That said, pollen allergies are more of a concern in temperate climates than tropical ones, and in very general terms smoking (usually of tobacco) is more common in temperate areas than tropical ones.

Contact with other populations is generally more common here than in other climates, as is urbanisation, and this can lead to urban-specific health problems. Disease and illness can spread faster in these environments due to crowding, and air pollution-related illnesses develop in societies with polluting technologies.

However, because temperate climates can support a vast array of foods, and because of the generally hospitable climate that avoids extremes, good health is common.

ART AND LEISURE IN TEMPERATE CLIMATES

Because temperate biomes enable a more communal style of living and have generally plentiful food sources, team games and sports are very likely to evolve here. In our real world, many ball games evolved in temperate grassland regions, and hockey-like games in particular evolved in many temperate regions.

Horses are a common and important feature of life in temperate biomes, and thus horse sports such as racing may develop.

Wrestling and archery are also common—hunting skills in general are important when grazing herbivores constitute a large part of the diet, and demonstrations of these skills can form the basis of leisure time.

Art and artistic expression is integrated into daily life. As with savannahs, there is little distinction between an artist and a craftsman, and beading, carving, weaving and painting are common forms of expression. Pottery is also a common art form, though it seems to be more common in forests and woodlands than in grasslands, possibly due to the higher incidence of nomadic cultures in grasslands.

COLD FOREST CLIMATES: BOREAL FORESTS AND NORTH-WEST CONIFEROUS FORESTS

Cold forest climates include both boreal and northwest coniferous forests (found only in the northwest coastal region of North America). Although these both have distinct features in terms of climate, plant life and animal life, they are similar in terms of the types of cultures that tend to form in them.

BOREAL FOREST BIOME

Also known as taiga biomes, boreal forests have low annual rainfall, bitterly cold winters, and mild summers that are just long enough to let the ground thaw properly. Temperatures are below freezing for at least six months of the year.

Precipitation falls as snow in winter, so while average yearly rainfall is low, the snowmelt in spring provides enough moisture for trees to survive.

However, because of the cold conditions and the usually-poor soils, trees are coniferous, with different varieties of needles rather than soft leaves. These needles are hardier and less able to be damaged by frost and snow, enabling the tree to photosynthesise year-round. They also lose less water during the day, allowing the tree to conserve its precious water supply.

Conifers native to boreal forests tend to be thin and upright so they can pack densely together, creating a warmer, slightly more humid microclimate. This shape also helps snow slide easily from their branches, rather than weighing them down and potentially breaking them.

The high density of trees has other flow-on effects: firstly, there is little in the way of an understory, as light can't reach all the way to the ground, and secondly, because the trees are packed close together and are often quite dry (due to the low annual rainfall), boreal forests can be susceptible to wildfires. These fires strip away the tops of the trees, often leaving the lower parts unscathed due to the extremely thick bark that most boreal trees have. This allows more light through, and there is a rush of growth as saplings compete for resources.

KEY BOREAL FOREST PLANTS

In milder boreal forests, some deciduous trees can survive, but for the most part the vegetation is exclusively coniferous, with only a handful of different species.

COLD FORESTS

Common plants include:
- Spruces
- Firs
- Hemlocks
- Pines
- Small, berry-bearing shrubs
- Many lichens and mosses

KEY BOREAL FOREST ANIMALS

Boreal wildlife includes:
- Predators such as lynxes, timber-wolves, weasels and relatives like wolverines and minks;
- Small herbivorous mammals such as squirrels, beavers, snowshoe rabbits and hares, voles, and shrews;
- Larger herbivores such as moose and deer;
- A wide variety of birds (woodpeckers and hawks to name just two).

Many of the birds migrate into boreal regions during its short summer, when the snowmelt makes the ground wet and swampy—the ideal place for insects to thrive, and a natural, seasonal banquet for insectivore birds.

COLD FORESTS

NORTH-WEST CONIFEROUS FOREST BIOME

This biome is very location specific. It occurs along the north Pacific coast of the USA and Canada, an area that would be part of the boreal forest biome except for the fact that it gets lots more rainfall because it's right next to the ocean.

The ocean also moderates the temperatures, so although it's still much colder than a temperate forest, it's warmer than the average boreal forest.

Did You Know?

The very existence of the North-West Coniferous Forest biome proves that these are all guidelines rather than fixed rules: here is a biome that would be one thing (a boreal forest), except for the fact that it breaks one key rule (in this case, by having lots of rain), and so it becomes another thing entirely its own.

Once you get comfortable with the 'real world' biomes and understand *how* climates affect their cultures, don't be afraid to experiment with things.

Of course, it helps to understand how biomes form in the first place, too. For that, check out *How To Map*, also in the *Inkprint Writers* series.

COLD FORESTS

Soils are generally rocky and acidic, and similar plants and animals are found here as in the boreal environment.

KEY NORTH-WEST CONIFEROUS FOREST PLANTS

Trees are usually coniferous. Common plants include:
- Firs
- Spruces
- Hemlock
- Redwoods (such as the famous giants)
- Mosses
- Dogwoods
- Rhododendrons
- Other flowering shrubs

KEY NORTH-WEST CONIFEROUS FOREST ANIMALS

Wildlife includes:
- Bears
- Elk
- Large deer
- Beavers
- Owls
- Bobcats
- Weasels and their relatives (pine martins, stoats, marmots, etc.)

COLD FORESTS

- Otters
- Birds such as woodpeckers, jays, songbirds, hawks

FOOD IN COLD FOREST CLIMATES

The cold and seasonably variable climate of cold forests (both boreal and north-west) means they are generally not suited to growing many common food crops. However, many native food sources are available; berries, in particular, are plentiful, especially blueberries and cranberries.

Wild mushrooms abound, fiddlehead ferns are common, and wild rice also grows. Wild mint, dandelions, some lettuces (such as miner's lettuce), watercress and sunflowers also all grow in this environment. Sugar maples thrive here, and birches, common in most boreal forests, provide a sweet sap that can be eaten in a similar fashion to maple syrup. Some pines also have an inner bark that can be ground and used as flour.

Hunting, trapping and fishing are also important facets of boreal food culture, with fish (such as salmon, trout and pike), deer, moose, elk and reindeer forming important sources of dietary protein.

Meat generally features prominently in the boreal diet, and large herbivores such as reindeer can be bred and herded for meat and hides. Birds

COLD FORESTS

that may be eaten are also common in summer, following the explosion in the insect population.

CLOTHING IN COLD FOREST CLIMATES

Most clothing in cold forest climates is made from animal hide, as plant fibres are not as insulative.

Footwear generally consists of boots of varying lengths, up to thigh-high, lined with fur and made from water-resistant leather.

Over-garments are generally parka-style coats, double layered for extra warmth and insulation, and decorated with beading for aesthetics, and fringes to help keep the wind out. Shorter coats and a loincloth over leggings could also be worn.

Head coverings are important in cold weather and are usually either fur hoods (particularly water-repellent furs such as wolf that can help prevent breath creating a build-up of frost) or, in

DID YOU KNOW?

Interestingly, the most recent studies have shown that the domestication of dogs probably occurred in boreal areas, contrary to the popular belief that domesticated dogs originated in the Middle or Far East.

summer, cloth squares folded around the head and draping down behind.

Woven cloth coats may also be used in summer if the population has access to either the raw plant materials or can trade with other populations.

SHELTER AND THE ENVIRONMENT IN COLD FOREST CLIMATES

Wood is obviously plentiful, so log cabins are the most common form of permanent housing.

More portable forms of shelter are tents made from reindeer or other large herbivore hides. These portable shelters enable herders to move with the herds to better grazing grounds during winter or summer as necessary.

Both cabins and tents must be designed to withstand snowfall, with slopping roofs so that snow cannot build up.

ECONOMIC DEVELOPMENT IN COLD FOREST CLIMATES

Travel in cold forests can be quite difficult, with snow to contend with in winter and dense brush all year round. Additionally, cold forests are often found near extensive wetlands, and can contain large bogs or swamps.

Water travel is preferred in many areas for these reasons (although snowshoes are thought to have been invented in boreal areas—no surprises there!), but the difficulty of travel and the extremity of the winter season can significantly limit economic growth.

Furs are a major export, with creatures such as reindeer, bobcats, foxes, wolves, rabbits and various members of the weasel family (wolverines, pine martins, minks, ermine, sables, stoats, etc.) providing thick, warm, highly prized pelts.

Iron and aluminium ores can be extracted from deeper soils.

Additionally, being a forest area, wood and other forestry products also provide significant exports—in many areas, the major exports.

In areas where they exist, reindeer can also be an important commodity for meat, antlers and hides.

Finally, many cold forests overlie significant deposits of natural gas and petroleum, as well as deposits of gold and diamonds, making mining an extremely important source of economy as well.

HEALTH AND MEDICINE IN COLD FOREST CLIMATES

A wide variety of herbal medicine techniques exist in the boreal forest biome. Among the most common medical complaints are:

- Skin conditions (mostly dermatitis, eczema and poxes such as chicken pox)
- Various injuries caused by the environment, including treacherous snow and/or boggy conditions
- Gastrointestinal complaints (including generic stomach upsets, but also cholera and dysentery)
- Fevers
- Musculoskeletal problems, including arthritis, joint pain and swelling, aches, strains, sprains, and so forth
- Tooth problems, which can be associated with scurvy (caused by a Vitamin C deficiency, which can develop with comparative ease, since cold forest climates rely heavily on meat—although it's by no means a foregone conclusion: see the 'Food in Tundra Climates' section)
- Eye conditions including snow blindness
- Respiratory concerns such as asthma, pneumonia, diphtheria and tuberculosis
- Urinary problems involving the kidneys, the bladder, or urinary tract infections

In many cold forest areas, populations believe that a gift must be left in exchange for a plant that is taken for healing or medicinal purposes, with the most commonly used plant being sphagnum moss, which is used as a dressing for bleeding wounds—entirely sensible given sphagnum moss's unmatched ability to absorb up to 4000% of its own weight in liquid.

ART AND LEISURE IN COLD FOREST CLIMATES

One of the most distinctive art forms to come from cold forests is birchbark bitings—the practise of biting patterns into the relatively soft bark of birch trees. The resulting pieces can be used as templates for beading and embroidery or kept as artworks in and of themselves. Birch bark is also a common material for weaving baskets and the like.

Beadwork, likely using bones or wood, and quillwork are common, with a slight trend toward floral designs. Stone carvings are relatively common, and jewellery is an important art form, often employing dried berries and dyed fish scales as well as the bone, teeth, claws and so forth common in other climates.

TUNDRAS

While tundra biomes experience permafrost (permanently frozen sub-soil), they are not covered by snow and ice year round. They have short, cool summers in which the top few inches of soil defrost and become waterlogged, and long, below-freezing winters in which this soil refreezes solid.

These harsh conditions cannot support trees, and more extreme tundras can't even support shrubs; because the soil is frozen, these plants can't access nutrients, and the constant melting and refreezing of the soil means that roots are alternately swamped by the melt and then crushed by refreezing ice.

Few plants at all can survive these conditions, which are also generally soil-poor and rocky. Interestingly, however, studies have found that the variety of microorganisms in tundra soils is greater than that of nearby boreal forests; researchers are still investigating why this may be so.

As well as the obvious location in the arctic circles, tundra-like biomes can also occur in alpine regions.

However, while extremely high mountains such as the Himalayas have true tundra biomes on their peaks, most high-mountain biomes are a mixture between true tundras and the biome that surrounds the mountains, commonly temperate woodlands or forests.

In alpine regions, frequent high winds, poorly-developed soils and short growing periods combine to stunt the growth of plants, often resulting in trees with short, twisted forms.

Tundras serve an important role in maintaining the overall climate and conditions of a planet; Earth's tundra regions are one of its three major carbon sinks.

Generally, plants take in carbon while they are alive and give it off as they decompose, but the icy conditions of tundra winters mean that plants tend to be preserved rather than decaying, so their carbon is never re-released (unless a massive climate event results in these tundra areas melting).

Did You Know?

'Carbon sinks' are areas that take in more carbon than they release and therefore help to maintain the balance of gases in the atmosphere. Too much carbon is bad, because it amplifies the sun's radiation and contributes to a warming global climate.

Earth's three major carbon sinks are the polar ice sheets, our oceans, and major forests.

TUNDRAS

KEY TUNDRA PLANTS

Few plants can survive in the tundra, but the ones that do are ground hugging: lichens, mosses, sedges, and short grasses.

KEY TUNDRA ANIMALS

True tundras have a surprising number of resident mammals, given the conditions. These include:
- Musk ox
- Arctic foxes
- Caribou
- Shrews
- Voles
- Hares
- Wolves
- Bears (including polar bears)
- Some deer
- Lemmings and other small rodents

Unsurprisingly, there are very few reptiles in the tundra biome, as it simply too cold for these ectothermic creatures. On Earth, there are a total of four frog species, one newt, and one lizard that can be found in tundra regions.

During the summer months, tundras often become marsh-like, making them a perfect home for insects such as:

- Mosquitoes
- Flies
- Moths
- Grasshoppers
- Blackflies
- Arctic bumble bees
- And more

This plethora of insect life attracts a vast array of migratory birds such as:
- Ravens
- Hawks
- Falcons
- Sandpipers
- Terns
- Snowbirds
- Gulls
- And more

Fish such as cod, salmon and trout are also found in the tundra biomes.

FOOD IN TUNDRAS

Because of the harsh nature of the tundra environment, there are very few edible plants. Some berry-bearing bushes can survive, and some greens and roots can be obtained in the warmer months.

TUNDRAS

Otherwise, meat forms the bulk of the diet. In coastal areas, fish are a significant source of nutrition, along with seals, walruses and whales, and crustaceans such as crabs and shellfish. Large land mammals such as caribou, moose and reindeer are also hunted (sometimes herded) for food, and migrating birds make a good meal too.

Somewhat surprisingly, given modern western health food advice, this high-fat, high-protein diet provides excellent nutrition for human beings, providing plentiful trace vitamins and minerals through the wide variety of meats, cuts and organs that are consumed, often only lightly cooked.

(This light cooking may be part of the secret, since vitamins in particular break down easily at high temperatures.)

Given these food sources, hunting is a vital skill.

Food preservation focuses on salting and drying in order to keep food through to the end of the harsh winter.

There are no trees for firewood in the true tundra, so food is frequently eaten raw or dried—though fires for light, warmth and cooking are created by burning animal fats and blubbers. Dried meats may be dipped into liquid or whipped fat or blubber to soften and moisten them.

As trade with other populations increases, cooked food becomes more common and foods from other biomes become more available.

Generally, though, food is only seasonally plentiful, so populations in tundras are likely to have a 'feast or famine' mentality, consuming food in large quantities when it's available to compensate for the times when there is little to no food.

(This can cause serious health issues once contact with other populations and steady trade routes become established, as age-old food culture meets processed and refined sugars and fats in plentiful supply.)

CLOTHING IN TUNDRAS

Again, because of the harsh climate and lack of sustainable plant life, most of the clothing native to the tundra biome is animal-based. The skins from the animals consumed for food provide much-needed warmth and insulation in the form of tents and blankets, as well as wearable clothes.

These clothes often take the form of thinner, fur-in layers against the body, followed by thicker, fur-out layers on the outside.

Bulky outer parkas may have fringes at the bottom to help keep the wind out, and hoods are often lined with water-repellent fur such as wolf or wolverine to help prevent a build-up of breath-induced ice. The parkas themselves are usually of a more common, easily obtained fur; caribou is preferred where available because it's supremely warm.

These coats must be removed when doing sweaty work; sweat can dampen clothing, leading to reduced insulation, frozen clothing, and potential frostbite, or worse.

On the lower half, knee-high fur-in leggings provide foot warmth and sweat absorption. These are often followed by fur-out shorts, topped by knee-high fur boots, and finally overshoes made from a waterproof skin where possible (seal is a good example).

Fur plays a vital role in protecting the extremities; even when they are available, commercially produced shoes and boots are unlikely to protect against frostbite as well as furs.

In the summer, sealskin is the preferred fur where it is available, as it is thinner and lighter—although it is extremely tough and requires tenderising in order to work with it, usually through the laborious process of chewing on it over the course of five to six days. (Yes, chewing, as in with your mouth!)

Unless other options are available by trade, there are no plants to provide thread, so animal sinew is used.

Metals, too, are extremely rare, and if they exist are tremendously difficult to extract from the ground, so carefully shaped bone shards form needles strong enough to penetrate fur.

As trade with non-tundra populations becomes more commonplace, furs are gradually replaced with commercially-made hiking clothing in most situations—though as noted, fur still reigns supreme in its ability to protect from frostbite, and so remains the preferred outer layer when living in extreme conditions for significant periods of time (for example, when hunting).

SHELTER AND THE ENVIRONMENT IN TUNDRAS

Although in modern times icehouses, or igloos, are used mostly only as overnight stays for hunters, they are much warmer than both tents and wooden huts. The snow insulates in much the same way as down does in sleeping bags: by trapping air (which is a poor conductor of heat) in its millions of tiny pockets, and therefore keeping the heat generated by human bodies and campfires inside the house. For longer term situations, tunnels are constructed at the entrance to keep out the wind.

In spring, when icehouses melt, tents made of skins are used instead. Because the tundra ground is usually frozen, it's difficult (if not impossible) to use pegs, so instead tents are constructed with flaps or pockets along their bottom edges, which are filled with rocks.

Bedding in both cases is provided by furs and hides, with synthetic materials creeping in as access to technology increases.

In some areas, populations may choose to overwinter in towns of a style more familiar in temperate climates, returning to the tundra in the summer months.

Permanent houses are unlikely to have more than a single storey; because heat rises, it's not energy efficient to keep a multi-storey house properly warm in a tundra climate.

Porches, however, are a virtual necessity as a place to store snow gear that would otherwise cause a mess; these items collect snow and ice that would melt as soon as it was brought into the warm house.

Houses must be built on blocks which are set on beds of gravel, or on metal poles drilled into the permafrost, otherwise the warmth from the house could melt the subsoil and cause shifting and subsidence.

Did You Know?

'Frost upheaval' is when the ground is forced upwards because water in the soil freezes. Ice takes up more room than water, remember!

Relatedly, frost upheaval and subsidence is common throughout autumn and spring respectively, so roads and paths in tundra areas are often made of gravel; gravel helps to prevent traffic areas becoming muddy and impassable, and has more flex than tar or bitumen roads, which would crack as the ice moves the ground.

MARRIAGE AND THE FAMILY IN TUNDRAS

The tundra environment is extremely hostile and requires that people band together for support. For this reason, populations in these areas usually place a great emphasis on sharing and hospitality. This extends particularly to food and shelter.

It is often expected that people can visit at any time, regardless of whether they know the family or not, and shelter and a meal will be provided. Cooperation, community-mindedness, collaboration, generosity and hospitality are not just values that grease the social wheels; they can, in some circumstances, be life-saving.

Also as a result of the harsh nature of the environment, both children and old people are respected and valued. Babies are often carried under a mother's parka until they can walk and run confidently themselves (in many societies, they will spend approximately two years relying entirely on their mother in public). This forms very close bonds between the two, and necessitates some spacing out of births.

In keeping with these communal values, multi-generational households are likely to be common, with older children and the capable among older generations pitching in with child care and house work.

Elderly people are also respected for their survival skills and general life knowledge, as surviving to any great age on the tundra is a feat of skill in and of itself.

ECONOMIC DEVELOPMENT IN TUNDRAS

Trade is primarily based on meat and furs, peaking in summer when the ice is at its lowest, allowing maximum contact with other populations.

Generally speaking, native populations in tundra areas will be nomadic, in order to follow their food sources.

It's virtually impossible to farm and extremely difficult to mine in such a climate, so economic systems are often based on trade and barter. However, money systems can be devised using bone or shell—or with metal, paper or plastic money if the population has significant contact and trade with populations in other climates.

Semi-permanent townships may spring up in the summer when conditions are better, and these will probably centre around the main points of contact with other non-tundra populations. These points of contact are either by land or, more likely, by sea, since sea travel is easier to guarantee than land travel in the tundra. This is where medical and educational institutes are also likely to be found, if they exist.

Where technology allows, fire stations are also a necessity, as such cold climates usually mean the air is quite dry, making indoor fires a threat.

The high value placed on cooperation and communal efforts make it a little more likely compared to other climates that populations will be ruled by elected representatives, or else elders who have proven their ability by the sheer fact of their long existence.

HEALTH AND MEDICINE IN TUNDRAS

In general, health afflictions revolve around the perils of ice and exposure, with frostbite, or worse, hypothermia, posing serious risks. Dehydration can also be a significant issue due to the extreme dryness of the air.

Sunburn is also common, as light reflects off all the ice and snow.

Snow blindness, a painful—though usually temporary—disorder of the cornea resulting from overexposure to reflected UV light, can occur easily, as can boils if skin is not cleaned properly or clothing does not adequately wick moisture away from the skin.

Accidents are another serious concern: snow-covered water may not be entirely frozen, snow that appears stable may be slushy, ice can cause slips, and avalanches may be a concern.

A lot of these concerns are offset by a native population's intimate knowledge of the workings of ice and snow, but accidents (and bad weather) still happen.

Finally, as exposure to populations in other climate areas and technology levels increases, tundra-based populations gain access to other food sources.

However, often these food sources are higher in sugars and unhealthy fats than the typical tundra diet. If we remember that typically, tundra populations eat on a feast-or-famine schedule, it's easy to see that over-consumption of these less healthy foods can be likely, ultimately leading to high incidences of heart disease, diabetes, and other diet- and weight-related issues.

TUNDRAS

ART AND LEISURE IN TUNDRAS

Artistic expression in tundra regions often takes the form of sculptures and collages created with the available natural materials.

Skins can be used as a backdrop for drawing and painting (and for musical instruments such as drums), but sculpture seems to be more common. It is often created using the clay found when the top few inches of soil defrost in the summer.

Time is often considered a flexible concept in the tundra, mirroring the flexibility of time shown in the environment: in a traditional round planet with ice caps forming at the poles, the tundra regions will have summer periods where the sun never sets, and winter periods where the sun never rises.

Because of this, populations rely on instinct and impulse to motivate work, eating, sleeping and play, rather than external environmental cues—leading to the sense that objective time is somewhat flexible.

Given the emphasis on survival, tests of strength may be popular. On the other hand, in a culture where survival is reliant on group cooperation, competitive sports are less likely to develop than in more gentle climates.

WATER BIOMES

Although the term biome is usually used for climate/vegetation/wildlife niches on land, it can also be applied to water areas as well.

The distinction between fresh and salt water is rather obvious, with fresh water being characterised as water that is less than 1% salt.

Salt water is by far the more abundant, making up about 96.5% of the Earth's water.

The remaining 3.5% is fresh, but over two thirds of this is locked up in ice and glaciers, and a little under one third lies below the surface as groundwater. This leaves less than 0.1% of all the Earth's water as both fresh and easily accessible.

Did You Know?

The salt in saltwater is composed of many, many different salts. There is regular table salt, or sodium chloride, but calcium carbonate, gypsum, magnesium chloride and potassium chloride are all common too.

Despite this, fresh, accessible water plays a vital role in sustaining life; not only does it provide hydration for most of the world's plant and wildlife species, it also acts as the basis of important biomes of its own.

WATER BIOMES

In fact, there are three biomes based in fresh water: ponds and lakes; rivers and streams; and wetlands.

Additionally, there are three salt-water biomes: oceans, which contain further zones; coral reefs; and estuaries.

Let's explore them each in turn.

WATER BIOMES

PONDS AND LAKES

Ponds and lakes can obviously differ greatly in their size, ranging from no more than a pace across, to great lakes the size of a small country. Because of this, the lake biome encompasses many different variations.

The larger the surface area of the pond or lake, the greater the species diversity will be. However, because their waters have little to no interaction with other water sources, many lake or pond species are endemic, which means that they are only found in one very particular location in the entire world.

So, while lakes have a much lower diversity compared to other aquatic biomes, they also have a high proportion of unique and uncommon species.

THE LITTORAL ZONE:
WATER LESS THAN 5M DEEP

Lake biomes can be divided into four zones. The topmost zone is the littoral zone, which includes water less than 4.5m/15ft deep. This is the warmest water zone, as it's comparatively shallow and energy from the sun can easily penetrate through the water.

Because of this, it hosts the greatest diversity of plant and animal life, as it's warm, accessible, and has the greatest supply of nutrients. Many terrestrial or land-based species rely on the littoral zone for a source of water and food.

KEY LITTORAL ANIMALS

Frogs, fish, turtles and snails are all common, as are crustaceans, molluscs, flatworms and insect larvae.

THE LIMNETIC ZONE: SURFACE WATER OVER DEEP WATER

The middle zone of a pond or lake is called the limnetic zone. Like the littoral zone, it includes surface water and is therefore well lit.

However, the littoral zone is a shore zone, while the limnetic zone is the open water in the middle of a lake or pond above the deeper waters. It extends down to the point where sunlight can't reach any more, and is dominated by plankton.

Fish may either be herbivorous, feeding on plant matter and plankton; omnivorous, feeding on particles of whatever nutrient-rich material they can find; or carnivorous, hunting other smaller fish for food.

WATER BIOMES

KEY LIMNETIC ANIMALS

Hundreds of fish species live in the limnetic zone, as well as small crustaceans and rotifers (nearly microscopic multicellular animals). Insects are also common, and plankton thrives here.

THE PROFUNDAL ZONE: DEEP WATERS

The lower zone is the profundal zone, which encompasses the deeper water of the lake. (Due to their shallowness, ponds do not have a profundal zone.) Life cycles in this bottom portion of water are primarily driven by nutrients that float down from above as sunlight doesn't penetrate this far into the water, and oxygen levels are comparatively low.

Particles of organic matter and minerals gradually sink, as do the carcasses of dead animals and dead plankton, providing a source of energy and nutrition for the creatures that live in this lower zone.

The temperature is stable at around 4C, or 40F—the temperature of an average refrigerator. In lakes where the surface freezes over in winter, the profundal zone may actually be the warmest zone during this season.

In spring, when the limnetic zone at the top of the lake is no longer being constantly chilled, the

WATER BIOMES

warmer water from the profundal zone rises and the waters of the lake become mixed. This mixing, encouraged by the wind, can also occur in autumn, and helps to turn over the nutrients in the lake or pond.

KEY PROFUNDAL ANIMALS

Leeches, annelid worms, some species of insect larvae including lake flies, and a few types of crabs and molluscs. There is little to no vegetation in this zone.

THE BENTHIC ZONE: THE LAKE OR POND FLOOR

Finally, there is the benthic zone, or lake floor. Like the profundal zone, life in this zone relies on nutrients floating down from above. In large lakes, life congregates around the carcasses that fall to rest, as these provide concentrated sources of nutrients.

Animals here fall into several categories according to the way in which they feed. Filter feeders use fins or other appendages to create a current that directs water through their mouths (or equivalents), allowing them to strain out nutrients. Examples of benthic filter feeders include lobsters, some crabs, clams, worms and sponges.

Grazers scrape or shred nutrients from other surfaces. Examples include insects such as mayflies and some water snails, and many fish, molluscs and crustaceans.

Deposit feeders ingest the silty sediment on the lake bottom indiscriminately, eliminating large quantities of waste product and digesting the nutrients. Examples include some water snails and shrimp.

Finally, some creatures are predators that generally lie in wait for hapless prey. In deep water, the comparatively low density of nutrients in this zone make the expenditure of energy expensive, so it's more efficient energy-wise to wait for the prey to come to you. Ambush predators include many species of flat fish, some freshwater stingrays, and some species of catfish.

KEY BENTHIC ANIMALS

Animal life in the benthic zone generally consists of crustaceans and other invertebrates, with the occasional fish species—usually a species with a flattened profile and eyes on top of the body to allow the fish to sink down into the sediment and wait for a meal (think sting rays, flounder, plaice, halibut and sole).

WATER BIOMES

KEY POND/LAKE PLANTS

Aquatic plants are lighter and more buoyant than terrestrial plants. Because they are partially supported by the water, rigidity is less important, so aquatic plants put their efforts into fast growth rather than woody tissue. However, because they can be buffeted by both wind and water, flexibility, as well as strength, is vital.

Common pond and lake plants vary according to region, but can include members of three categories:

- Free floating plants, which, as their name suggests, float freely on the water's surface (duckweeds, floating ferns, water hyacinths, watermills, and more);
- Submersed plants, which are plants rooted in the sediment and entirely covered by water (pondweeds, naiads, parrotfeather, coontail, various grasses, and more);
- Emergent plants, which are rooted in the sediment but extent out over the water's surface (lotuses, water lilies, water willows, alligator weed, water primrose, rushes, sedges, and more).

WATER BIOMES

RIVERS AND STREAMS

Streams and rivers vary wildly in characteristics along their length. Broadly speaking, they can be divided into three zones: the source or headwaters, the mouth, and the middle. The source or headwaters zone is the coldest, most oxygen-rich part of the stream, and fish species like trout thrive.

The middle zone of a river is the most species-diverse; the river or steam is wider and the increased sediment load (the amount of dirt, silt and other particles that the water is carrying) provides more nutrients for both plant and animal life, which in turn provides more food for larger animals. Algae and other aquatic plants begin to appear, as do various water insects in stagnant or slow-flowing pools along the river's edges.

In the mouth section of the river, the sediment load is heaviest and oxygen levels are lowest. In very large rivers, the mouth section can be so full of sediment that the water appears muddy (this can occur in middle sections too) and the fish life consists mostly of species such as catfish and carp that require less oxygen and little light. Obviously, river systems are extremely diverse, and one river system can be almost entirely different from another.

The major factors that impact the river biome are speed of flow, amount of light penetrating the water, temperature, water chemistry and substrate (what the river is flowing over).

Rivers and streams are also home to migratory species.

Freshwater fish are physiologically different from saltwater fish. Fish living in salt water can easily exchange the internal salts of their body with the salts in their environment.

However, since freshwater fish can't rely on their watery home for salts, they are adapted to ensure that their body salts remain where they belong: inside their bodies. Because of this, their gill structures are more complex, their scales are thicker to reduce salt loss through their skin, and they have better-developed kidneys that help prevent too many salts from being lost in their waste fluids.

Migratory species, then, must be able to survive in both types of environments, which can be difficult physiologically. This is why many species that migrate between salt and freshwater environments do so at different life stages: their different physical forms at different ages allow them to adapt to the differing demands of the biomes.

Eels, salmoniformes (such as salmon and trout) and sea lamprey all have different levels of tolerance to salt water during their various life stages.

WATER BIOMES

KEY RIVER/STREAM ANIMALS

Common wildlife in river and stream biomes include:
- A vast variety of insects;
- Molluscs such as snails, limpets, clams and mussels;
- Crustaceans such as crayfish and crabs;
- Amphibians such as salamanders and frogs;
- Reptiles such as snakes, turtles, crocodiles and alligators;
- Various bird species such as ducks, geese, kingfishers, cranes, egrets and herons;
- Mammals including otters, beavers, hippos, river dolphins and platypuses.

Naturally, fish also abound, varying widely depending on the characteristics of the river. However, freshwater fish generally spend much of their time either at the bottom of the river or in pools out of the main current, as swimming in the main current expends a tremendous amount of energy.

KEY RIVER/STREAM PLANTS

Vegetation includes:
- Lilies
- Lotuses
- Water cress

- Mosses
- Sea grasses
- Rushes and sedges (near the edge of the water)

A tremendous variety of trees, determined by the surrounding biome, also thrive along the river edge with its easy access to water. Algae and plankton, which are not plants, but rather tiny organisms, also populate river systems.

WATER BIOMES

WETLANDS

Wetlands encompass a variety of wet zones that can vary depending on their local climate. For the purposes of this book, we'll consider 'wetlands' to include all freshwater areas that are neither lakes, ponds, or rivers, and 'estuaries' to include both salt water wetlands, and wetlands where salt and fresh water meet.

There are two ways of talking about wetlands. First, we can describe them in terms of the dominant plant life:

- Swamps are wetlands dominated by trees, such as the cypress swamps that make up the bayous of Louisiana and Florida in the USA.
- Marshes are wetlands dominated by grasses, such as the Kakadu Wetlands of northern Australia.

Alternatively, we can describe wetlands by how they are formed:

- Bogs are wetland areas created when a lake fills in, often with mats of sphagnum moss and other floating vegetation.
- Fens, on the other hand, occur when ground water seeps up from below and creates a wetland area.

The type of plant life in a wetland will depend on the wetland in question. However, in general you can expect the same types of plants that you would find in pond and lake environments. Some bogs, fens and marshes will be dry enough to permit a multitude of grasses, ferns, and other typically land-dwelling plants to flourish.

Sphagnum moss is one plant commonly found in all sorts of watery environments, but particularly in bogs. Interestingly, one of the side effects of an abundance of sphagnum moss is that it makes the water acidic. This significantly reduces the volume of bacteria in the water and slows or completely prevents the process of decomposition. This means that things which fall into this water tend to be preserved, rather than rotting away.

However, because things that fall in are not rotting away and releasing their nutrients back into the environment, the water in sphagnum-moss-rich areas is often low in nutrients, particularly nitrogen, which is an essential nutrient for most plant life.

The only other easy source of nitrogen in a sphagnum moss bog is insects, so where there is a lot of sphagnum moss, there are also often many carnivorous plants, such as sundews and pitcher plants.

In contrast, fens are usually alkaline rather than acidic, which means berries thrive here. Fens are covered with peat instead of with sphagnum moss.

WATER BIOMES

KEY WETLAND PLANTS

Common species in bogs include:
- Poison sumac
- Water lettuce
- Cypresses that have pneumatophores (the spongy wooden structures that grow up from their roots above the surface of the water to allow their roots to receive oxygen, often colloquially known as 'Cypress knees')
- Lilies
- Leatherleaf
- Sphagnum moss
- Maples
- Swamp roses
- Sawgrass
- Horsetails
- Sundews, pitcher plants and other carnivorous species (especially where there is lots of sphagnum moss)

Fens, being more alkaline, tend to be home to species such as:
- Bluestem grass
- Indiangrass
- Tamarack
- Poison sumac
- Bog birch
- Many sedges and grasses
- Some pitcher plants

- Cranberries
- Blueberries
- Peat moss

Notably, rice is often farmed in wetland areas, not only because it requires a lot of water, but because flooding rice fields keeps competing weeds at bay. Sometimes, these flooded fields are used to raise complementary crops or stock (such as crayfish) when they are not in use for rice.

KEY WETLAND ANIMALS

Although species vary according to location and type of wetland, in general they are similar to what might be found in ponds and lakes.

Some examples could be:
- Amphibians, particularly frogs, and newts;
- Birds, such as grebes, herons, kingfishers, pelicans, and more;
- Fish, including perch, carp, bream, cod, suckers, tilapia, bullheads and hardyheads, etc.;
- Insects, particularly mosquitos, who require standing water to breed, and leeches, who also prefer standing water, but also dragonflies, dampers, butterflies, ladybirds, pond skaters and aphids;
- Mammals such as beavers, minks and muskrats;

WATER BIOMES

- Reptiles such as alligators, turtles and snakes.

WATER BIOMES

ESTUARIES

Estuaries, like wetlands, are zones where water and land meet. However, unlike wetlands, estuaries contain salt water, as they form where fresh and salt water meet. The nature of the estuary, then, is heavily influenced by the nature of the river that feeds it.

If the river is large and consistent, then the estuary will be relatively buffered from the seasons and lower in its salt content. On the other hand, if the flow of the river or stream changes seasonally, the concentration of salt will be higher during the dry season and lower during the wet season.

Regardless, plants and animals must be able to adapt to both salt and fresh water environments. As mentioned in the river biome section, freshwater fish are physiologically different to saltwater fish, possessing more complex kidneys and renal systems, more complex gills, and often more sturdy scales. Possessing the features necessary to survive in both environments is difficult, hence why migratory species that pass through both salt and freshwater areas often do so at different stages of their lives.

However, many animals do thrive in the complex estuary environment, and many fish species find them a particularly suitable nursery, particularly estuaries that have consistent salinity levels.

Plants too must adapt to high levels of salinity that are usually considered toxic for them. Some plants, such as pickle weed, have developed the ability to store salt in pockets in their leaves called vacuoles.

Others, such as salt grass and alkali health, have the ability to 'sweat' salts out through the porous surface of their leaves, a process that often leaves them covered in a fine coating of salt crystals.

KEY ESTUARY PLANTS

Mangroves can create estuary swamps in tropical areas, but generally the types of plants found in most estuaries include:
- Various seaweeds
- Sea rushes
- Saltwort
- Ribbonwoods
- Shore primroses
- Pickle weed
- Grasses including salt grass

Few trees thrive in the estuary environment due to the salinity, but common species include mangroves and Hudson estuary trees.

WATER BIOMES

KEY ESTUARY ANIMALS

Fish that thrive in an estuary environment include:
- Carp
- Sticklebacks
- Flathead
- Bream
- Whiting
- Tailor
- Herring
- Sprats
- Breeding bass, snapper, halfbeaks and tarpon
- Mudskippers
- Archer fish
- Migrating salmon

The shallower waters of estuaries are also often home to huge numbers of invertebrates, including:
- Mussels
- Prawns
- Shrimp
- Oysters
- Crabs
- Worms

These invertebrates are a veritable buffet for a variety of wading birds, such as:
- Cormorants
- Ibises

- Ducks
- Sandpipers
- Terns
- Spoonbills
- Egrets
- Herons
- Oystercatchers

Other common animals include:
- Migrating geese
- Seahorses
- Sea turtles
- Rays of various kinds
- Some sharks
- Jellyfish
- Sponges
- Eels

WATER BIOMES

OCEANS

Like lakes and ponds, the ocean is divided into several different zones. In this case, the zones are:
- intertidal
- pelagic
- benthic
- abyssal

Very different plants and wildlife can be found in each of these zones, as different characteristics are needed to survive.

THE INTERTIDAL ZONE: SHALLOW WATERS

The intertidal zone is where ocean and land meet. The water is shallow enough for sunlight to penetrate all the way to the sea floor, and the sea floor may even be completely exposed at low tide. This area supports a diverse array of molluscs, plants, crustaceans and small fishes.

Because of the significant influence of the tides, intertidal zones tend to be organised in vertical layers according to how much or how little water each of the various life forms require. In rocky areas, these layers are obvious; in sandy or muddy areas, the sea floor is stirred by the tide and so the layers are not as distinct.

Additionally, in sandy or muddy areas, algae and seaweeds find it harder to establish themselves, as the seabed is constantly in motion. For these reasons, rocky shores have a much greater diversity of life than sandy or muddy shores.

KEY INTERTIDAL SPECIES

Intertidal species are often species that can be found in rock pools as the tide retreats. Common species include:
- A variety of bacteria and fungi;
- Coral, anemones and jellyfish;
- Sponges;
- Sea stars, urchins and cucumbers;
- Crustaceans such as shrimp, crabs, lobsters and many hundreds of insect-sized species;
- Molluscs such as whelks, snails, mussels, periwinkles, scallops and barnacles;
- Cephalopods such as octopuses, squid and cuttlefish;
- Small fishes such as blennies, the long-spined sea scorpion, lumpsuckers, rock gobies, and butterfish;
- Many seaweeds, such as kelp, Neptune's necklace, and more;
- Red, green and brown algae of many forms and varieties.

WATER BIOMES

THE PELAGIC ZONE:
SURFACE WATERS OVERLYING DEEP WATER

The pelagic zone is the upper section of the ocean out away from the shore – the open waters down to about 200m.

Sunlight penetrates throughout the pelagic zone, so plankton, algae, and surface seaweeds thrive. Correspondingly, so do many fish and mammals that feed on plankton and algae, as do the fish and mammals that feed on the other fish and mammals.

Most of the pelagic zone is water only with no sea floor. Because of this, it is quite featureless and unvarying, which in turns leads to a low level of species diversity.

This zone is well lit, allowing predators to use their eyesight to hunt down prey. Unlike in other zones, predator fish and prey fish have generally similar body shapes: a deeply forked tail and a smooth, gently tapering body that tapers roughly equally to the head and to the tail.

This body shape is the most energy efficient, enabling pelagic fish to conserve energy and, in many cases, reach incredible speeds—the Indo-Pacific sailfish, for example, can sprint at over 110km/hr.

It's also a more effective shape for swimming long distances, something many fish species in the pelagic zone do regularly, either in the general course of hunting for food, or in seasonal migrations.

The lack of general scenery has two other results. First, there's little to hide in or under or behind, so many fish in this zone have a silvery colouring that helps camouflage them with the surrounding water, usually darker on top and lighter underneath.

Secondly, any objects that are found floating around in this zone—sea weeds, drifting flotsam, even large fish or jellyfish or divers who stay in the water for long enough—tend to attract a crowd.

Probably this is because hiding out near a larger object can provide some protection, at least for the smaller or younger fish (sea turtles being used as a shelter by smaller fish have sometimes been speared by swordfish who weren't aiming for them), but possibly it's also out of sheer interest; the verdict isn't in on that one yet.

KEY PELAGIC SPECIES

Many hundreds of species thrive in the pelagic zone, such as:
- Plankton species;
- A wide variety of algae;
- Surface or floating seaweeds;
- Mammals such as whales and dolphins;
- Predatory fish such as tuna, barracuda,

sailfish, swordfish, marlin, flying fish, trevally, bonito, mahi-mahi, mackerel and kingfish;
- Jellyfish of a wide variety of shapes, sizes and colours;
- Deep-sea rays and many sharks, including apex predators like the Great White;
- Large filter feeders such as basking and whale sharks;
- Other fish such as herring, sardines, sunfish, sprats, anchovies, whiting and more.

THE BENTHIC ZONE: DEEP WATER

The benthic zone lies beneath the pelagic zone. Some light filters down, but it is a dim twilight, rather than bright sunshine.

The sea floor is included in the benthic zone where the ocean isn't too deep, and many forms of seaweed can be found here.

This zone is quite rich in nutrients, as a lot of particles float down to this zone from the pelagic zone above, especially when plants and animals die.

Fish in this zone are in near constant contact with the sea floor, and as such the vast majority of species are either ambush predators, or 'sifters' who roam over the sea floor, searching through the silt for food. These sifters search for their food either by physically sifting through the sea floor, or by using other senses, like the hammerhead shark searching for the electrical signature of stingrays buried in the sand.

KEY BENTHIC SPECIES

The benthic zone supports a huge array of life, including:
- Many fish, such as haddock, catfishes, flat fishes (flathead, flounder, sole, etc.), gobies, darters, and rattail fish;
- Rays and hammerhead sharks;
- A variety of bacteria and fungi;
- Coral, anemones and jellyfish;
- Sponges;
- Sea stars, urchins and cucumbers;
- Crustaceans such as shrimp, crabs, lobsters and many hundreds of insect-sized species;
- Molluscs such as whelks, snails, mussels, periwinkles, scallops and barnacles;
- Cephalopods such as octopuses, squid and cuttlefish.

In addition to this, there are a variety of creatures that are classed as 'benthopelagic', which means they swim freely between the benthic and the pelagic zones. These include:

- Deep-sea cod
- Deep-sea eels
- Many sharks, although not at the deepest reaches of the benthic zone
- Deep-sea rays
- Patagonian tooth fish
- Orange roughies

THE ABYSSAL ZONE: THE DEEPEST OF THE DEEP

Finally, the abyssal zone consists of the deepest parts of the ocean. The water at these depths is close to freezing temperature and is under immense pressure. Oxygen levels are high, but nutrient levels are very low as most nutrient-rich particles have already been filtered out of the water by creatures living in the pelagic and benthic zones.

There is no sunlight at all in the abyssal zone to provide energy, so most life congregates around hydrothermal vents—places where superheated water and/or magma break through the Earth's crust from below, bringing new nutrients. These vents provide warmth and food for chemosynthetic bacteria. These are bacteria that create energy from chemicals in the hydrothermal vents, rather than creating energy directly or indirectly from the sun.

A variety of invertebrates and fishes then eat the bacteria (and each other).

Some sea life does exist in the abyssal zone apart from these hydrothermal vents, of course. Usually these creatures have their own light organs of some kind, for communicating with others of their species (we presume) or luring in prey. Fish at these depths are often terrifying and monstrous in appearance, with huge, narrow teeth and oddly shaped bodies.

KEY ABYSSAL SPECIES

Not many creatures have what it takes to survive the intense physical pressure, lack of constant nutrient supply, and (unless they live around a vent) icy temperatures of the abyssal zone.

However, some creatures that not only manage to survive, but thrive here, include:
- Dumbo octopus
- Deep-sea lizard fish
- Hagfish
- Giant tube worms
- Angler fish
- Glass squid
- Giant sea spiders (a type of crab)
- Vent crabs
- Deep-sea bamboo coral

WATER BIOMES

- Vent limpets
- Vent mussels
- Scale worms
- Brittle stars
- Other sea stars

WATER BIOMES

CORAL REEFS

Coral reefs form in warm waters, most commonly within 30 degrees either side of the equator, and there are three types:
- Fringing reefs build outwards from rocky coasts
- Barrier reefs form parallel to the coastline and block off large coastal lagoons
- Atolls form as reefs completely enclosing a lagoon in which there is no dry land.

The ocean-facing side of each of these reefs receives a steady supply of plankton and nutrients from deeper water, and so has the most growth. The lagoon sides have soft floors, consisting of sediments that get trapped by the reef, and often boast luxurious sea meadows. These sheltered sides provide the ideal habitat for many of the reef species.

Corals, the most important reef creature, are actually animals related to jellyfish and anemone. If you can imagine a tiny anemone that secretes calcium carbonate (limestone) that solidifies into a cup around it to act as an external skeleton, you'd be basically on the right track.

And just like anemones can withdraw their tentacles, corals can hide in their calcium carbonate cup when they feel threatened. These tiny coral polyps usually mass together, building vast and beautiful structures that form the basis of the coral reef.

Corals also have a symbiotic relationship with certain species of algae, which means that the two species exist in a relationship so close that neither one would survive as well by itself. These microscopic algae species live in the gut of the coral and can photosynthesis sunlight into sugars. The algae not only make enough for themselves, but because they are protected by the coral, they make enough left over sugars for the coral.

This is an important source of nutrition for the coral, as the crystal-clear water around the reef is usually so clear precisely *because* there are very few nutrients floating around in it (such as plankton and bits of dead plant and animal).

Nonetheless, with the help of their symbiotic algae, the little coral polyps are able to gain enough nutrition to survive. They supplement the sugars the algae provide by stinging and reeling in small prey like anemones and jellyfish do, or by constantly filtering seawater and extracting any little bit of nutrition they can.

As well as the microscopic algae in the coral, larger algae species grow near reefs, often in the form of turfs. Just like above-water turfs, these algae turfs can form vast, beautiful meadows that are a food source for many other creatures. Most notably, long-spined sea urchins graze on the turf, opening spaces for coral larvae to settle and helping to increase the biodiversity of the reef. Green sea turtles and manatees or dugongs also feed on these sea turfs.

KEY CORAL REEF ANIMALS

Coral reefs are home to a huge array of creatures. Most common are invertebrates and fish.

Invertebrates include:
- Sponges
- Anemones
- Nudibranchs
- Limpets
- Urchins
- Sea stars
- Sea horses
- Brittle stars
- Sea cucumbers

Many thousands of fish species also make their homes in coral reefs. Unlike corals, which are often endemic (unique to their particular area), reef fish are often global in their distribution. Herbivorous reef-dwelling fish include:
- Damselfish
- Parrotfish
- Surgeonfish
- Clownfish

- Anemonefish
- Goatfishes
- Moorish idols
- Angelfish
- Cleaner fish, including wrasses

A handful of fish species actually feed on the coral itself, including:
- Butterflyfish
- Triggerfish
- Pufferfish

And larger predatory fish, drawn in by the huge numbers of smaller, herbivorous fish, are common too, including:
- Snappers
- Groupers
- Squirrelfish
- Barracudas
- Garfish
- Mullet
- Reef sharks
- Rays

MOVING FORWARD

By now, you should have a good idea of the kind of culture you'll end up with, depending on what sort of biome your population lives in.

This is a good moment to stop and point out one of the saddest worldbuilding crimes: that of over-simplification.

Star Wars, though a classic in many respects, is one well-known science fiction text that's guilty of over-simplification: although whole new planets are introduced, they seem to be homogenous, with just one climate and one culture spanning the entire globe.

However, this is just not scientifically possible (keep an eye out for *How To Map*, another *Inkprint Writers* title, to find out why!). To compound that, it's not fair, either, because resorting to monocultures is what creates and reinforces stereotypes.

The science fiction novel *Feed*, by award-winning author M. T. Anderson, puts it beautifully as the main character discusses the planet Mars with his friend. "Yeah, I've been to Mars," the narrator informs us. "It was dumb." His companion laughs. "Are you serious? ... Mars is a whole planet."

Precisely. How can you possibly write off a whole planet with a one-word description?

MOVING FORWARD

Never forget: If you're working with a whole planet, then you need a whole planet's worth of cultures.

...Which, of course, is why I don't recommend working with a whole planet. You'll drive yourself to distraction trying to establish all said cultures, and end up spending far too much valuable time worldbuilding instead of actually creating your story or game or campaign or whatever your final product is.

Instead, I highly recommend that you save yourself a lot of effort and focus only on a couple of key locations, using your knowledge of biomes to emphasise a couple of key differences between your populations—just enough so that your readers understand that you, clever you, are *not* going to write off an entire planet with one generic description, and that you (basically) know what you're doing.

Remember, the end goal here is to actually write your book or develop your game, etc, not to lose yourself in months and months of worldbuilding, no matter how much fun that might be!

PART TWO: TECHNOLOGY AND CULTURE

We've talked now about the ways in which the climate and geography of an area are likely to affect populations that live there. However, there is another critical factor that shapes the characteristics of your population: the level of technology your society has access to.

While the ways that technology impacts cultural development are many and varied, with tiny difference in the starting conditions sometimes creating huge differences down the track, it *is* possible to draw some generalisations.

In studying the development of western cultures, demographers noticed that, once societies settle down to agriculture, they often follow a similar pattern to each other. This pattern is called the demographic transition timeline, or just the demographic transition.

This theory reflects the development of western cultures in particular, and doesn't account for the impact of globalisation (which can cause societies to skip stages entirely to 'catch up' with their neighbours) or the fact that various locations in the one country can be at different stages of the timeline simultaneously.

PART TWO: TECHNOLOGY & CULTURE

However, as a starting point for building your own cultures, it's an extremely useful paradigm to be aware of, providing a basis for your invented culture's politics, economics, family dynamics and more. It can help you to consider how the level of technology a culture has impacts more than just their ability to travel fast over long distances, or mass produce clothing, etc.

Just remember that, like anything which involves people or a complex system (and cultures are both!), there are no rules, just guidelines. I'm not setting out to describe exactly what has happened in all cultures throughout Earth's history; I'm trying to give you a rough idea of what you could expect your fictional culture to look like and why.

So, with those caveats in mind, what is the demographic transition?

There are five key stages on this transitional timeline, and each stage is defined by three factors: the population's birth rate, the population's death rate, and the corresponding overall change in population levels.

STAGE ONE

In the first stage, birth rates are high, and so are death rates. This stage is often the longest and focuses on the period of pre-industrial agriculture.

PART TWO: TECHNOLOGY & CULTURE

(Note that hunter-gatherer cultures fall outside the scope of the demographic timeline, which focuses on how the development of *agriculture* specifically impacts a culture.)

In this stage, there is no technology beyond basic tools, and death rates are high. This is due to the lack of industrialised medicines and hygiene practices, as well as the frequent warfare and conflict that cultures in this stage experience as they fight to obtain or defend resources.

The birth rate is high—higher in agricultural cultures where a labour force is required than it is in hunter-gatherer cultures, in fact.

Women in farming communities tend to have as many children as they are physically able to (although herbal birth control, selective abortion and a variety of cultural practices such as living apart from male partners for a period of time after birth allow them to space children out). However, because the death rate is correspondingly high, population growth is very slow, if there is any at all.

Famines, plagues and invasion are the biggest threats to population in this stage, and families are large and intergenerational.

STAGE TWO

In the second stage, death rates begin to decline. Historically, this has been mostly due to agricultural practices such as seed drilling and crop rotation that have secured a consistent food supply (fewer people die of starvation, one of the main causes of death in Stage 1). Improved health and hygiene practices also help to reduce child mortality through reducing the spread of disease (another major contributor to the high death rate in Stage 1).

However, the second stage of the demographic transition is still characterised by high birth rates, as there is both a real need to have many children to help out with family work and finances, and a perceived need to have lots of children to compensate for infant mortality (even though this is dropping due to improved hygiene). Because of these factors, this is the period when a population sees the fastest growth.

Later in this period, industrial technologies begin to appear.

STAGE THREE

In the third stage, population increase begins to slow. Contraceptive technology is more readily available, but more importantly, attitudes towards fertility begin to change. Often this stage is accompanied by increased urbanisation, brought on by the population explosion from Stage 2 and the need for a larger urban labour force. This

PART TWO: TECHNOLOGY & CULTURE

increases the cost of raising a child while diminishing their potential financial contribution to the family, and families everywhere 'realise' that they no longer need to have extra children to account for child mortality.

Importantly, women receive greater access to education and paid (or more highly paid) employment in this stage of transition, and this significantly impacts the number of children a woman is both willing and able to raise.

Therefore, this third stage is characterised by falling fertility rates and low death rates.

Technology blossoms, and by the end of this stage, communication technologies allow near-instant communication around the world; this is especially the case if the other nearby populations are already in Stage 4 of the transition.

Even in the earlier parts of this stage, though, infrastructure expands and becomes more sophisticated: flight becomes possible, dramatically decreasing the perceived distance between places around the world and the accessibility of trade, and space travel emerges as a feasible possibility.

Generally, while parts of society become disillusioned by industrialisation and are fighting against the increasing mass-production of goods, the attitude towards technology is positive.

Together, industry and technology make many promises about what they can and will deliver, and people are amazed and astounded at the things they are seeing created.

STAGE FOUR

The fourth stage of demographic transition is characterised by a low birth rate, and also a low death rate. Most so-called 'developed nations' today sit in this fourth stage. The population levels are high overall, but are reasonably stable.

Healthcare and disease prevention give rise to longer life expectancies, and technological advances can play a part in extending life.

Birth rates are low due to increasing opportunities for women outside childbearing, and a societal awareness of the importance of fatherhood as well as motherhood emerges. Couples may choose to abstain from having children at all as, in this stage, the 'family' is being redefined and children aren't needed as a source of labour in the home. Often this is because many tasks that once had to be done at home, such as food and clothing production, are now outsourced to corporations, and these processes may have in turn been largely automated.

Technology becomes integrated into society, changing the way that people interact and creating a truly globalised world, both in terms of economy and social awareness. While the initial response to this sudden boom in technology tends to be negative, with a lot of dooms-daying as the technologies arrive with a host of new social paradigms to navigate, the incorporation of technology into daily life becomes unavoidable, and opting to live a fully 'manual' or 'off grid' lifestyle where every need is catered for directly by family members is extremely difficult.

STAGE FIVE

In the fifth stage, birth rates continue to fall until they are below replacement levels, and the population begins to shrink.

There seems to be a link between increased wealth and significantly decreased birth rates, presumably because of the fact that higher education and wealth are linked and higher education (particularly of women) corresponds to lower birth rates.

In this stage, service and research jobs (as distinct from primary industries and manufacture) are dominant, and technology pervades all aspects of life. The workforce is highly mobile and flexible, but this also leads to long work hours and social dissatisfaction, often resulting in high divorce and suicide rates, as well as poor mental health, high levels of stress and stress-related illnesses, and over-consumption in many areas of life.

PART TWO: TECHNOLOGY & CULTURE

Whether or not this is *inevitable*, we can't be sure: only a few populations have made it to Stage 5 so far—but so far, these observations hold true, and given the nature of humanity, there is a certain logic inherent in them. Given there is so little data available about Stage 5 populations at this point, however, we will not be including them in our discussion here.

Because of all this, decisions you make about your society's level of technology are more loaded than you might think. Not only does each level of technology bring its own paradigm with it, but it also determines the degree to which the population's environment is *able* to impact its culture; the more technologically advanced and globalised a population is, the less likely it is to be constrained by its geographical factors. It's also much more likely to skip through the stages of demographic transition quickly, whereas the populations on your planet at the forefront of technological development will move through the stages relatively slowly.

It's important at this point to restate that many of the generalisations of the demographic transition are drawn specifically from western populations—and not only that, but western populations that used plough-based agriculture

PART TWO: TECHNOLOGY & CULTURE

for much of their history (with or without the help of animals). This lends an undeniably western slant to the discussion that follows, and although by comparison the specific distinction of *plough-based* western societies may seem trivial, the influence of the plough is also greater than you might imagine—see Stage 1 Family and Marriage for the discussion on how and why the use of the plough is linked to systemic gender inequality.

The other important thing to note is that, despite the assumption of most populations through most of history that technological development equals progress equals good, and that 'contemporary' (by any population's standards) is not just preferable to but *better than* 'old-fashioned', there is a significant body of evidence to suggest that improved technology does not actually lead inevitably to better health and lifestyle outcomes. This observation extends right back to the dawn of agriculture, with evidence suggesting that, despite our instinctive assumptions, general human health took a significant plunge when we moved from hunter-gathering to settled agriculture.

Thus, when we talk about moving 'along' the demographic transition timeline, let it be known that there should be no aspect of value-judgement involved; a Stage 4 society is not 'better' than a Stage 1 society, and a Stage 1 society is not 'worse'

PART TWO: TECHNOLOGY & CULTURE

than any of the others that come after. Humanity is, after all, humanity, and there are problems and advantages at every stage of human development.

So, with all that in mind, let's have a look, at how each of these different technological stages affect the development of culture.

Remember, once again, as we travel through these stages that these ideas are generalisations; there have always been, and presumably always will be, populations that for some reason or another are the exception to the norm.

STAGE 1

- High birth rate
- High death rate
- Pre-industrial agriculture
- Slow population growth, if any
- Key threats: famine, plagues, conflict

FOOD

In Stage 1, food (its production, preparation and consumption) is one of the central concerns that motivate populations. These societies are pre-industrial, so agriculture is low-tech.

In early Stage 1, food will consist entirely of what can be grown locally. Variation will be highly seasonal, with fresh pickings slim in the winter months and populations relying on stored food to see them through. In these scarcer months, meals may be highly repetitive in terms of both preparation method and content.

Families will be large, due to the high birth rate and the need for help to sustain the family, which means more food is required—but cooking can be time-consuming and laborious, especially without the aid of timesaving technology. Because of this, food preparation and consumption are likely to be significant and respected.

STAGE 1

Food is likely to be a bonding experience shared by the family or community, though communities will be comparatively small, with their size constrained by the amount of food that can be locally produced.

While canning isn't an option until later stages (post industrialisation) and iceboxes are far too expensive (except in icy climates!), in Stage 1 food can still be stored for leaner months through drying, salting, smoking, fat-preserving, pickling, and by turning raw produce into forms that will keep longer, such as alcohol, cheese, and jams or jellies. Homes will have to facilitate this food storage with cool rooms or cellars, or food can be stored in sheltered holes in the ground or in running water to keep it cool. Household gardens are common.

CLOTHING

Even in pre-industrial societies, it is likely that your population will use clothing of some sort—especially if there is snow! Cotton, linen and silk have been spun, woven and dyed since prehistoric times, and animal hides have been common almost everywhere at one time or another, as have various 'wools' made from the hair of whichever animals are most accessible.

Needles might be made from bone, wood or metal later in this stage if it's easily available.

STAGE 1

Early forms of clothing in moderate climates are generally simple. Often, they are just a full width of fabric draped around the body and either roughly stitched or belted into place. Warmer climates might use a simple loincloth, while cold climates will obviously adapt with layers of clothing made from animal fur or skin.

Buckles, pins and buttons made of natural materials (shell, wood, bone, etc.) could also be used to secure clothing.

Because Stage 1 clothing is still very simple, men often wear tunics, kilts or other skirt-forms that fall to the knees, and women tunics or dresses of some kind. In the later parts of this stage, breeches (pants that end fitted at the knee, and may be loose and billowy above) or other simplified trousers may become common for men. Although some cultures in this stage could use buttons to do up their clothes, a lot of populations make do with simple ties—they're much easier to make.

In temperate areas, sleeves aren't likely to appear until later in this period; the earliest tunics are nothing more than two rectangles sewn or tied together at shoulders and sides. If standards of modesty and protection from extreme cold or heat (more closely linked than you might think!) mean some sort of covering for the arms is necessary, shawls or cloaks may be used. Footwear for both men and women is generally soft leather tied with laces or straps.

Standards of modesty are usually linked closely to the area's climate. Forcing everyone to cover up from neck to ankle is impractical and unlikely in wet tropical areas, while in desert cultures, full-coverage clothing provides sun protection, so stricter standards of modesty are more comfortably enforced.

Sun protection in desert climates aside, there's definitely a marked tendency for cooler-climate

Did You Know?

A lot of social norms develop to keep people safe in their environments, not just norms relating to modesty. For example, many farming communities have developed injunctions against eating bulls and/or pigs: bulls pull the plough, and so are needed in order to ensure the on-going fertility of the farm, so it makes sense to avoid eating them. Likewise, pigs use a lot of water and are a vector for many diseases that can also affect humans if the meat is not thoroughly cooked, so injunctions against pig meat also make sense in early farming contexts—or, indeed, in later-stage contexts where factory farming can result in meat that may be contaminated by disease vectors and broad-spectrum antibiotics.

cultures to have stricter standards of modesty compared to populations in the tropics.

Because Stage 1 populations lack electronic and transportation technology, populations have to rely on nearby resources to create their coverings. Some trade may be available, but the fabrics or hides imported from other places will generally be extremely expensive and therefore highly valuable in society.

So what kinds of fabrics will populations likely use? It depends on their climate!

Cotton grows best in hot, humid climates with lots of rainfall.

Wool can be used anywhere suitable for grazing sheep (or goats or camels or any other creature with suitable hair) and has the benefit of being a

DID YOU KNOW?

Although in modern cultures we are used to walking so that our heels strike the ground first, for most of history people walked toe-first. This is because their shoes weren't as sturdy and thick-soled, and walking toe-first minimises the risk of accidental injury (consider how you might mince through a patch of prickles, for example). Neither way of walking has been found to be 'better' than the other, apart from the risk of stepping on foreign, potentially painful, objects.

fantastic insulator, meaning it keeps you cool in summer and warm in winter.

Flax and other reed fibres (used to make linen) grow best in temperate climates.

Silk comes from silk worms, which feed on mulberry leaves, a deciduous tree found in temperate climates. Interestingly, silk worms aren't found in the wild, but are a domesticated species (estimates suggest that they were first domesticated around 2600 BC in our world), something that can be a great source of conflict as regions seek to protect the secret of silk production.

Basically, clothing can be and has been made from any fibres available in the surrounding natural environment, so revisit your culture's biome and consider what they have to hand.

Due to limited resources, labour-intensive processes, and the expense of creating clothing, most people in Stage 1 societies don't own multiple outfits, or if they do, they likely have one, maybe two sets for everyday wear and one 'good' outfit for special occasions.

Dye colours are based on natural substances and richer, brighter colours are harder to make, which means that they are usually reserved for the wealthy and privileged. Dyes come from clays, plants, animals, and insects.

Common dyes might include:
- ochre, derived from iron-rich clay;

STAGE 1

- madder, a rich red-purple derived from the root of the temperate-zone madder plant, that can make a range of colours from orange through to burgundy;
- indigo, a dark blue derived from a variety of tropical plants (and historically important as blue dyes were extremely rare);
- cochineal or carmine, a crimson-coloured dye made by crushing the cochineal insect or its eggs (still widely used in food dyes and lipsticks), native to semi-arid regions;
- Tyrian or royal purple, derived from the mucous secretion of predatory sea snails in temperate oceans (and extremely valuable because instead of fading, this dye grows brighter and more vivid with exposure to sunlight);
- kermes, a red dye (less bright than carmine, although kermes is actually the original of the word carmine) also derived from insects, but more widely available as these insects live in temperate regions; and
- woad, a blue dye (weaker than indigo) derived from a plant of the same name that is found in steppe and semi-arid zones.

Decorations for fabrics and clothing can be either printed (often wood block printing), painted (especially on silk, which was also used for

STAGE 1

writing in early China), embroidered, or decorated with embellishments such as feathers or beads.

SHELTER

Some Stage 1 societies can be nomadic. Housing in these societies is likely to be portable or easy to reconstruct at each stop out of nearby materials: bark huts, skin or woven fabric tents on poles, and earthen floors. It's unlikely that these houses will be divided into rooms. Instead, there might be separate shelters with occupants divided by gender, family, age, or any combination of these. Shelters might have internal fires for cooking and warmth, or fires may be external to the housing and cooking done in the open.

Otherwise, houses are likely to be simple, with few room divisions, and constructed out of local materials with earth floors and minimal facilities, usually built by the owner and friends or relatives.

Kitchens commonly rely on open fires in a cooking space (which might also be external to the house in an attached room, or completely separate to keep the heat out of the house and reduce the fire risk), and bathrooms are more likely to be outhouses (pit-style, unless globalisation or extreme innovation has made plumbing available) that are often shared between a few families or even the whole village.

STAGE 1

A three-room set-up is probable: a sleeping area, a cooking area, and a communal area—although sometimes the cooking and communal areas are the same space. The whole family (likely including extended family and other ring-ins) may share a single sleeping space, and woven mats, straw-stuffed mattresses and simple blankets or some combination of these could constitute a bed.

In well-forested areas the house itself is likely to be constructed of wood, and the same wood could provide material for furniture. In other areas, any cheap and easily-sourced, local material will be used—think stone, adobe mud, daub-and-wattle, or even earth-berm houses.

More expensive housing for the rich might begin to display multiple storeys and may use heavier, more durable and more expensive materials in the building that might have to be imported. They could have flagged or paved floors, and bathing facilities are likely to be more permanent than just a bucket or pitcher and basin: individual baths may exist for private use, or communal bathhouses for use by the wealthy only may provide similar facilities.

FAMILY AND MARRIAGE

In very early Stage 1 populations, men's and women's roles tend to be relatively similar. The

STAGE 1

segregation between "men's work" and "women's work" actually *increases* as populations progress further into Stage 1, and particularly into the second and third stages. Believe it or not, this is largely influenced by the kind of agriculture the society practices.

Research has shown an extremely strong correlation between plough-dependent farming and lower female participation in work outside the home—and, correspondingly, attitudes of gender inequality, such as the idea that men have more 'right' to a job, or that they make better leaders.

The evolution from agriculture to entrenched sexism develops like this:

Working a plough (with or without the help of an animal) requires high levels of upper body strength, grip strength and raw power; it's also less compatible with childcare, meaning that for the most part, ploughing is a man's job. With the man of the house out in the field ploughing all day, it falls to the woman to run the household. This becomes entrenched over the course of a few generations, and it becomes normalised and expected that the man oversees the public sphere, and the woman is in charge of the private sphere.

At this point we're dealing with social norms that are not so much sexist as they are merely restrictive: men's work and women's work are likely to be considered equally valuable and necessary, but it's difficult for men to cross into running the private sphere, and women into the public sphere.

Discrimination enters the equation when families begin to band together to govern their settlements.

Forming a government, however loosely that term is interpreted, is something that happens in the public domain, so in a culture where it is firmly established that men run the business and women run the home, it is easy to see how the task of governing ends up with the men.

Add to this again several generations of reinforcement, and gender roles become not only stereotyped, but enforced. Because it's the way things have always been done, the assumption becomes that this is the only way for things to be done. Witness the circular logic, that assumes that men are naturally better suited to public leadership (etc.), because all women have ever done is run the home, so clearly women are unsuited for the task of governing, because they've never done it, while men have done it and are therefore clearly more suitable to continue doing it.

In contrast, cultures that trend towards shifting agriculture (gardening, or farming using labour-intensive devices such as hoes and digging sticks rather than capital-intensive devices like the plough) demonstrate much higher levels of gender equality. Both the average man and the average women can competently tend a garden and operate a hoe or a digging stick, regardless of personal physique, and it's entirely possible to competently mind children while performing these activities, so roles are less likely to be segregated by gender: both men and women operate in both public and private spheres.

Moving on to marriage and families more generally, you have a fairly wide range of options when it comes to age of marriage, and it will largely depend on the age your culture considers people to have become an adult at. In Earth's history, the range has generally been from 14 to 20.

Families are as large as physically possible for the practical reason that raising a child to adulthood in a Stage 1 society costs very little more than the food they will eat, while the potential benefit in returns to the family are high.

Children in this stage are depended on for child-minding; carrying water, firewood and messages; and various household tasks such as cooking and cleaning. Additionally, as children grow older they are able to become key players in the family 'business' of food collection and preparation.

In many pre-industrial societies, having lots of children is quite literally the parents' insurance

STAGE 1

against old age: if a couple grow too old to work for their own food without children to depend on, hunger and early death are likely.

Attitudes to these elderly members of society can vary drastically. Some cultures might revere their old people as valuable sources of knowledge; others may look on them as a drain on resources. Insofar as we can tell, there's no accurate way to predict which way a population will go with this, although the general availability of food and the value placed on knowledge and learning are certainly two key factors.

ECONOMIC DEVELOPMENT

The relationship between demographic stage and the type of economy the society will have is complex, but it also turns out to be somewhat predictable.

Populations with large proportions of either very old or very young people (ageing or growing populations) need to spend a lot of money and resources on caring for people who have no direct way to contribute to the economy, and this slows down economic growth.

In contrast, populations with a large proportion of working-age people, such as in a Stage 1 society, often have stable economies, because most of the population is contributing to it.

STAGE 1

Interestingly, most Stage 1 societies throughout history have been autocratic: either a true autocracy (often called a dictatorship), or a monarchy, or an oligarchy (which is like a dictatorship but with the ruling shared between a small group of people). Scholars think this is probably because other forms of government aren't really a priority when mortality rates are high, and when searching for food and shelter are people's biggest concerns.

Although Stage 1 societies have a large percentage of working adults and so are often reasonably stable economically, this stability is tied very closely to food availability—so closely, in fact, that in the 1790s, Thomas Malthus proposed the idea that economic and population growth were *always* tied to food. If the world could only produce 100 units of food, he reasoned, then populations could only grow so far before there just wasn't enough food to go around, and people would die.

His theory has long been disproved, but in his defence, this is exactly what populations in Stages 1 and 2 do, going through 'boom and bust' cycles as the food increases and decreases. So: in Stages 1 and 2, your population size will be limited by food availability. However, as they move into later stages, expect food to be less of a constraint.

One important consideration if you're building a Stage 1 society is what they will use for a 'money' system. History shows that there will be

STAGE 1

some kind of system set up: all but the very earliest societies used some form of currency exchange. Often this was just a fluid barter culture that allowed private exchange of goods in addition to exchange for currency, but it was clear to populations early on that true and exclusive barter systems suffer from several significant flaws:

- Finding someone who both has what you want and wants what you have is difficult and time consuming;
- Products may have spoiled by the time a 'buyer' is found;
- Various types of produce are not available at the same time during the year (for example, a grain farmer would find it difficult to directly barter with a fruit farmer).

Instead, various items that would remain stable and desirable for most of the population for most of the year are substituted: usually metals or, in areas where metals were not readily available, other precious but reasonably plentiful materials such as shells—or even paper money in the case of China. So-called 'Trading Post Economies' are also found, where items for trade are stored at a central location and managed by a central keeper.

Remember too that although Stage 1 populations are pre-industrial, this doesn't mean that there aren't any organised industries, or people with specialised occupations (although a signif-

STAGE 1

icant, rapid increase in the proportion of the population involved in specialised labour is one indicator of industrialisation).

Rather, 'pre-industrial' simply means that the economy is based mostly on primary production: farming, livestock breeding, and sourcing/refining natural resources.

HEALTH AND MEDICINE

While we take it somewhat for granted these days that disease is caused by germs—bacteria, viruses or fungi—for most of history, people didn't believe in germs. They were simply too small to see, and the idea of tiny, invisible creatures running around causing mayhem seemed almost like invoking a new kind of religion.

In fact, although the first germ theories were put forward in the 1500s, none of them really took hold until Louis Pasteur proved the existence of germs in the 1860s, when much of western society was already well into the third demographic transition stage.

So, instead of germs, health and medicine in Stage 1 societies are likely to be entwined with both religion and magic systems, resulting in a medical system that is both more personal and more holistic than contemporary western medicine (if objectively less effective).

STAGE 1

Disease and illness are significant causes of the high death rate in Stage 1 populations, particularly for infants and the elderly, so medicine and healthcare are integral parts of daily life in a more visceral way than in later demographic stages. This is best illustrated in the realm of religion: many of our world's religions include rules which seem utterly arbitrary on the surface, but which may in fact have been injunctions with health benefits—for example, many religions' taboos about touching the dead.

Because of all this, in Stage 1 societies particularly prayer and sacrifice are likely to play a significant role in healing, as are rituals.

And instead of germs, depending on the specific religious beliefs of the culture, disease might be seen as:

- A natural consequence of a particular action (don't do this thing or you'll get sick, ranging from abstract—"Don't offend the gods"—to specific—"Don't eat funky mushrooms");
- A result of travelling in a particular way or to a particular place (e.g. don't climb the mountain or the mountain spirits will be offended and you'll get ill);
- A punishment meted out for misbehaviour (you broke this law or custom and now you will pay);

STAGE 1

- A trial or test of will and endurance (you must suffer through this illness to prove your worth).

In public, religious officials, whether priests or prophets or witch doctors, are likely to be in charge of healing, using herbs as remedies and supplements and presiding over various 'cleansing' rituals. These rituals may actually be somewhat effective in that they often revolve around clearing the stuffy air out of a residence, or requiring the ill person to be bathed, or other such

DID YOU KNOW?

Although a high death rate is characteristic of Stage 1 societies, if you wanted to have a low-tech society with reasonably successful medicinal practices and thus a lower death rate, the most important factor you would need to account for is hygiene (and you'd likely be looking at small, probably transient or semi-permanent settlements with access to a varied diet).

Although it seems obvious to us that cleanliness can help prevent infection and the spread of disease, for a culture that doesn't believe in germs this connection is not obvious at all. Instead, the need to be clean would have to be accounted for in some other way—probably religion, or at the very least a set of inviolable cultural doctrines.

'cleansing' practices with (now) obvious health benefits.

However, the private, day-to-day care in these societies is often in the hands of women. Most early herbalists in the real world were female, and there are strong connections between old-culture witch mythology and female healers, with public (male) authority figures often being suspicious of women's knowledge and expertise in this domain. However, the knowledge passed on through this sector can be tremendous, with a true wealth of medical understanding and applied botany.

ART AND BEAUTY

Art has been around as long as we have—consider cave paintings, the earliest evidence we have of the human creative impulse. Well-developed creativity, like complex logic, sets humans apart from other creatures. And in fact, art fulfils a similar role in society to language: it's a concrete, tangible expression of abstract ideas and concepts, such as belonging, ownership, life and death. So really, it's no wonder that humans have always been interested in art.

The very earliest physical evidence we have for art, in fact, extends back before Stage 1 populations to true hunter-gatherer cultures. This

STAGE 1

evidence consists of some significant collections of reddish pigments, found preserved at sites of cultural significance across several continents (largely Africa and Europe). For a long time, archaeologists were baffled by these collections; they could determine that the pigments had been collected by women—which, they thought, made sense, since women, being the non-hunters, had more time to collect and refine these pigments. However, they were stumped as to what the pigments had been used for.

Some more recent studies, though, have suggested that these pigments were used for the very earliest forms of art: body art, particularly used by women to signal menstruation.

Stage 1 art is certainly not restricted to body art and cave painting, however; when you consider that Great Britain was in Stage 1 until the mid-1700s, it quickly becomes apparent that there are a plethora of artistic options available to populations in this stage according to the materials available in their biomes, so feel free to let your imagination run wild.

STAGE 2

- High birth rate
- Declining death rate
- Improved food supply and hygiene
- Fast, even explosive, population growth
- Key threats: social instability, unemployment, starvation

FOOD

In Stage 2, mechanised agriculture becomes widespread. However, the lack of widespread technology still makes both growing and preparing food time-intensive tasks. The flip side of this is that food-related activities are likely to still be highly valued by society, since they're both vital to survival and take a lot of time and effort to do.

(This also means that being able to afford to pay someone to prepare your food for you is a luxury and a status symbol.)

Remember to consider carefully what 'mechanised agriculture' will look like in your chosen climate zone. Temperate regions are likely to develop what we traditionally think of as farms (often before other populations—temperate societies are frequently among the earliest populations to move through the demographic stages, precisely *because* of their farm- and food-friendly climate), but in other climates, this 'mechanised agriculture' stage is going to look different.

In rainforests, it has historically often meant clearing of trees to make way for tropical crops, while in deserts it has often meant the creation of expensive infrastructure to provide water to crops. However, neither of these are a foregone conclusion.

It is entirely possible to 'farm' in desert regions without drawing prohibitively from the water table, providing the community is farming native plants that can thrive in desert conditions.

Likewise, it's entirely possible to 'farm' tropical zones without extensive tree clearing by using permaculture solutions that mingle shade-loving mid-height plants in amongst the tall rainforest trees, by encouraging 'groves' of useful trees that can still act as natural habitat, and so forth.

The reason that historically we've seen mechanised agriculture become destructive is because generally speaking, populations in Stage 2 don't have access to the kind of long-range data required to help them understand *why* practises such as deforestation are a poor long-term investment.

In addition, once mechanisation kicks in (and even more so when populations hit an industrial revolution in Stage 3), efficiency becomes a primary goal, and the agricultural landscape is physically transformed to make it easier for the machines to do their jobs. This feels an awful lot like progress, until the long-term effects begin to make themselves known.

However, as noted above, it's entirely possible to have a Stage 2 community 'farming' in a way that doesn't destroy their natural environment. To do this, you'd need to either have a way for your population to access the long-range data about the effects of destructive agricultural practices (e.g. a close relationship with a neighbouring population that has already been there, done that), or you'd have to give them a set of fairly inviolable culture practices relating to balance and harmony with their environment; nature-based religious practices would be (and have been) effective here.

Okay. Back to eating food, rather than talking about making it.

Meat in most climates is still going to be a precious commodity in this stage; higher socio-economic groups will enjoy the majority of it, while poorer groups are much more likely to eat a plant-based diet, supplementing it with animal produce that they can make themselves. Of course, in climates where plant matter is harder to find, the opposite will be true.

Because advances in agriculture mean more food can be produced, populations can start to form larger groups, which also makes land ownership even more important—particularly if it means

STAGE 2
Did You Know?

Much of what we consider to be 'cuisine' these days evolved from working-class food. Pizza, pasta, curries, and most other foods that evoke instant connotations of a particular culture or place were originally the everyday food of the masses by necessity, because they relied upon ingredients that could be grown and produced locally and cheaply. Often, they were meat-free or contained only minimal meat, due to the expense of meat in most climate regions. It was only later, once these cuisines became internationally desirable, that attempts were made to 'class them up' by incorporating more significant portions (or better cuts) of meat.

the difference between fertile land and infertile land. This can consolidate any class stratification that may have begun in Stage 1, with the upper class owning the land and the lower class or classes being forced to work it, or with wealthier people owning the fertile land and poorer people owning the less fertile land.

(it's worth considering how class structures are likely to develop in a climate where all land is equally fertile, or equally infertile; instead of land owner-ship, class structure may be based on something else, like trade skills or hunting prowess, age or leadership opportunities.)

STAGE 2

This increase in available food is one of the key factors that pushes a society from Stage 1 to Stage 2, since more food means more people eating which means fewer people dying of starvation.

It's interesting to note, though, that the most recent evidence suggests early Stage 2 farmers in particular suffered from poorer nutrition and shorter life spans than their hunter-gatherer and pre-industrial farming ancestors.

Partially this could be that higher densities of people in larger Stage 2 settlements allowed disease to spread faster, but it also has to do with the fact that farming tends to concentrate on a high proportion of meat and simple carb crops (rice, wheat, etc.), diminishing dietary variety and consumption of trace vitamins and minerals. People are eating more food overall, but with less variety and quality, providing calories at the expense of varied nutrients—a trend that sadly continues right through all the stages.

(Consider what you might need to change in order to address this in your fictional culture!)

Despite these theories, it's true that due to various advances in transport in Stage 2, people can travel longer distances, which means food can be imported more easily.

This can increase the range of food available, and the seasons it's available in—for those who can afford this gourmet food, at least, with foreign or fancy or out-of-season dishes becoming status symbols for the wealthy.

CLOTHING

Breeches (short trousers fastened just below the knee), pantaloons (long, baggy trousers drawn in at the ankle) and finally trousers (the full-length, tailored leg-clothing we are more familiar with today) have tended to become more common for men in temperate climates in this stage, because technological advances mean that it's easier to make more complicated clothing. If you have a temperate-climate population, you could go the trouser route, or you could complex-up your clothing in some other manner—let your imagination soar!

However, as with all new inventions and styles, in populations where trousers are not widespread or are still in the early stages, they're likely to be treated with suspicion.

Historically in this stage young children often still wear dresses, although in most cultures the style of dress for boys and girls is different.

In temperate climates, women's clothing is likely to still be floor length, as women's primary functions remain in the private, rather than public sphere, and as such their modesty and sexual purity is likely to be considered valuable.

STAGE 2

In addition to all this, the rise of trade between cultures (something that often begins with the cultures in the temperate climates, since they have better access to the raw resources needed to create the technologies that allow for travel, etc.) and better weaving technologies are likely to lead to more ornate fabrics, sometimes with rich and intricate patterns.

Knitting is also likely to become more popular in this stage, with the invention of both better technology and better stitches. In our world, the invention of the purl stitch enabled knitted fabrics to be made in the flat, rather than made in the round and cut open, while spinning wheels developed further, and the first looms began to appear.

In the later parts of this stage, as the industrial revolution approaches, both knitting and weaving are likely to become mechanised, and in the final stages sewing machines of some form are likely to appear, allowing for ever-more complex clothing designs. Generally, both fabric and clothing become more and more intricate, complicated, detailed, and better constructed.

Mechanisation, allowing for fast, mass production, also shifts the task of fabric creation from the home to the factory.

Upper classes (if they exist: not all climates are conducive to this—see the comments in the Stage 2 food section) are likely to wear silk, cotton,

STAGE 2

bleached linen, and dyed or simply-patterned wool that's of better quality and/or is harder to obtain (both equalling 'more expensive') than the every-day clothing worn by everyone else.

This every-day, everyone-else clothing will be made from whichever fabric is cheapest—usually made from local materials, often home- or locally-made.

Despite all these generalisations, in Stage 2 clothing styles tend to diverge and take on local styles and flavours—due to climate requirements, available technology, and cultural preference. In most places, though, there are enough resources for people to own a couple of sets of clothing, and the idea of having formal and informal clothes might start to become common. Embroidery can be quite common and popular, especially for formal wear, but also for everyday clothes, as individuals (usually females) are likely to have the skills to add this to clothing themselves.

It's also important to remember that despite all these tendencies, globalisation can quickly accelerate a Stage 1 society to a Stage 2 society by making trade and importation/exportation much more readily available. Clothing in particular can be affected by this, and national dress can be quickly replaced by commercially-manufactured clothes, even while the population itself is still in the second stage, because mass-produced and im-

STAGE 2

ported synthetics can wind up being cheaper than local, natural fabrics.

SHELTER

For climates and cultures that encourage social classes (see the comments in the Food section for Stage 2 above), shelter becomes one of the key ways to distinguish status.

Most people will likely live in small, cheaply-built houses built using local materials, similar to what is found in Stage 1.

In later parts of this stage, more complicated furniture may appear; metal (often iron) stoves might be installed as cooking fixtures in areas that have easy access to metals, and non-earthen floors begin to become more popular even among the average citizens, as do multi-storey buildings.

FAMILY AND MARRIAGE

Given the still-high birth rate, there's still a lot of emphasis on women's role as mothers in Stage 2 societies. However, their level of participation in the workforce will largely be a result of the type of agriculture the population practices (see Family and Marriage in Stage 1 for the full discussion about why).

STAGE 2

In populations that practice shifting agriculture, some historical estimates have placed female participation in work outside the home (which in this stage is, by necessity, almost exclusively limited to food cultivation) at a staggering 72% prior to the Industrial Revolution. This is in contrast to significantly lower numbers for women in plough-based agricultural populations.

However, in a real-world context, it's also important to note that historical data often didn't include women, not because they *weren't* working outside the home, but because recording that work wasn't considered important.

The textile industry is one particular example of an industry run almost exclusively by women prior to the Industrial Revolution, with spinning and lace-making particularly designated as 'female' jobs. Additionally, most working-class women didn't have the 'luxury' of conforming to the gender conventions of the upper class, and thus took whatever work was available to them (generally this was still work of a home-based nature, but there are records of women traders, apprentices and artists as well).

There doesn't seem to be any real way to predict whether a population will choose plough agriculture or shifting agriculture (and populations may switch methods as they move into Stage 2, often

STAGE 2

conforming to the practices of populations around them, particularly if the surrounding populations are in a later stage of the transition), so you're free to choose this as you wish. Just be aware that the decision you make here will have long-lasting effects throughout the population's existence because of its impact on gender roles and expectations.

As for families, they are likely to be even larger in this stage than in Stage 1, because most of the deaths that constitute the high death rate of Stage 1 occur before the age of five.

Once the factors that lead to this high death rate (unhygienic conditions and insufficient or inconsistent food supplies, as well as social conflict) are removed, maternal and infant death slowly go down, and the many children a woman might have are usually able to survive to adulthood.

This is seen as a positive thing, as children are still seen as valuable assets around the house. However, the growing emphasis on men's roles in the public sphere and thus the need for them to be educated may begin to draw male children away from the home, and in some cultures a preference for male children over female children might develop—especially if one's ability to earn a higher income relies on work outside the home.

Once again, at the opposite end of the age spectrum, the ways that all of this change impacts

STAGE 2

a culture's attitude towards its old people varies; however, attitudes to marriage remain relatively similar to those in Stage 1. Because a woman is expected to work inside the home and to bear as many children as she can (and because in some cultures female young adults might begin to be seen as a burden), women are encouraged—and often expected—to marry young.

However, because men are expected to provide financially for their family, and usually now require some sort of formal education to achieve this, men abstain from marriage until they're financially independent, leading to a marked difference in the relative age of the marriage partners, with women marrying in their mid-teens to early twenties, and men in their mid-twenties to... well, any age!

Unfortunately this also contributes to male-female inequality, as the female marriage partner is often significantly younger than her male partner, and thus more inexperienced, less knowledgeable, and generally less world-adept, reinforcing the perception that females generally are therefore weaker than males—further reinforced by the large number of widowed women (because their husbands were all older and have died off) who must be looked after by their children (because they are still not allowed into the public domain to earn income).

STAGE 2

Did You Know?

A 'failed' population is one that disintegrates to the point where it is no longer recognizable as a single cultural or national identity—or, to put it more simply, a population where the governing body collapses and can no longer control its territory, provide public services, interact representatively with other states, or wield the authority needed to make collective decisions.

ECONOMIC DEVELOPMENT

Of all the demographic stages, Stage 2 is where populations are most likely to fail. A lot of this is because of the way the age structure of the population changes. The high birth rate and declining death rate mean that the population quickly becomes 'bottom heavy'—there are lots of children and young adults in comparison to the rest of the population.

As noted in Stage 1 Economic Development, this means that there is a high proportion of the population using its resources without directly contributing to its economy, resulting in a slowing down of economic growth.

If this imbalance is also coupled with insufficient food and fresh water supplies, pioneering studies conducted in the 1990s suggest that the

STAGE 2

population has a massive 40% chance of degenerating into civil conflict.

Other studies conducted since the 1990s have not only supported this conclusion, but have also demonstrated that it's virtually impossible to create a stable, democratic population in Stage 2. The 'youth bulge' is, apparently, incompatible with democracy, particularly when said 'youth bulge' consists of males who (since the population is rapidly expanding) will likely find it difficult to get work.

So, to make sure that your Stage 2 population survives (assuming that's what you want!), what do you need?

First of all, a stable government that's capable of making laws and enforcing them.

Secondly, this government needs to make laws on specific topics to control the potentially negative effects of a rapidly increasing population:

- public health
- family planning
- education
- economics (esp. savings, trade and labour)

If the government can successfully navigate its population through these areas, then the population has a good chance of surviving.

Money-wise, things are likely to continue in this stage in much the same way as in Stage 1.

STAGE 2

However, storehouses for gold and other precious currency are likely to develop—which is to say, banks are invented. This also means that people can now use banknotes—bills issued by the bank to certify that you do in fact have enough currency to pay and which can be redeemed for currency. Often, in the latter end of this stage, national banks can take on the role of money printing and distribution, and the process is likely to become formalised in an attempt to prevent 'bankruptcy', or everyone cashing in their banknotes at the same time and depleting the bank's stores.

Finally, this is the stage where class structures are likely to become entrenched, particularly for populations that went the plough route for agriculture. Consider: societies before Stage 1 (that is, hunter-gatherer societies) are defined by a lack of stored and/or concentrated food sources. This makes it exceedingly difficult (not impossible, just more difficult) for an upper class to arise, because being upper class depends upon your ability to seize food and resources from others—something obviously facilitated by an ability to store food, and concentrate its production in herds, orchards, etc.

Agriculture is also the first step toward colonisation, because land use now becomes more strictly linked to land ownership—and in the real world, it's always been agricultural populations

STAGE 2

that forced nomadic or hunter-gatherer populations out of the best land, the land capable of *sustaining* a nomadic or hunter-gatherer lifestyle in the first place.

Now, all these tendencies exist in Stage 1, but because the populations are small and steady, the effects are negligible *on the Stage 1 population* (different story if you're one of the pre-Stage 1 societies being forced out of your homeland). It's when these populations hit Stage 2 and the population begins to grow rapidly that the impact of these changes really make themselves known.

Also, if you're dipping in and out of this book, it's worth jumping back to read the discussion in the Stage 2 Family and Marriage section about labour and the role of women when you're thinking about economic development.

HEALTH AND MEDICINE

In Stage 2, the death rate rapidly declines. Mostly, this is to do with improvements in hygiene and medical practice.

Most people still won't believe in germs because they're too small to see, but people are willing to accept that basic hygiene such as hand washing does seem to improve things and prevent the spread of disease.

STAGE 2

Religion is still important in medicine in this stage. It's most common for societies in this stage to believe that illness is a curse from their deity/deities, either through ill luck or as a consequence of rule breaking.

However, people still also believe that contemporary medical practices have much to offer in the way of treatment. While recovery from illnesses is invariably considered a favourable sign from the heavens, the role of doctors and healers in achieving and promoting this favour is still invaluable.

Also characteristic of this stage is a much more communal approach to medicine, perhaps facilitated by the fact that medicine and religion (often including magic and the supernatural) are so heavily intertwined.

The division between lay people and specialist practitioners can often be unclear, and in many places on Earth for many centuries, doctors were considered just one in an array of available medical options that might also include healers, druggists, herbalists and more. Medicine is considered quite literally just another discipline, one that the public have as much right to as any specialist. Medical concepts can be debated by the public, and it's likely to be extremely common for people to self-treat, or for people to treat themselves after or in consultation with a trained doctor.

STAGE 2

ART AND BEAUTY

Throughout history, standards of beauty have been inextricably linked to external signs of wealth. As well as the commonly desired features of health and youth (which are favourable from a reproductive point of view), cultures also tend to admire and desire the kinds of bodies available to the rich.

In Stage 2, the stage where agricultural developments are the most influential and much of the population is involved in food production in some way or another, the wealthy are those who can afford to pay others to work to produce food for them for them. Only commoners must work outside in the sun all day in order to eat, becoming sun-tanned.

Commoners are also likely lean due not only to hard physical labour, but also food scarcity.

Aristocrats, on the other hand, can afford to sit out of the sun in their mansions; they don't need to worry about where their next meal will come from, and so will often have a softer, more rounded physique than the labourers, with paler skin

DID YOU KNOW?

Some historical accounts suggest that European men first began to wear their hair short after Francis I of France accidentally burned his hair off with a torch.

untouched by long hours in the sun. This is more applicable, of course, in biomes that are conductive to class divisions—not all biomes are as readily able to support a few people sitting back and letting others do the work (though human laziness and greed being what it is, where there's a will there's a way).

Regardless, though, in a society where food scarcity is common, a physical appearance that suggests plenty is attractive—and a well-fed, well-rounded woman is also more likely to both survive childbirth and have offspring which are more likely to survive.

This is also the reason why fainting was considered trendy for women in the upper aristocracy in many places around the world: being frail and yet alive was a sign of significant wealth, because you could afford for other people to take care of you (whereas if you were poor and frail, you died).

Thus beauty; now for art.

Unlike in Stage 1 where art and craftsmanship are fairly synonymous, and everyone owns at least something that could be considered 'art' due to the high levels of skill and workmanship involved in the creation of everyday items, in Stage 2 as class divisions begin to really make themselves known, art becomes a luxury item. Because of this, art is often reflective of the lifestyles of the rich,

STAGE 2

rather than representative of societies as a whole, particularly since it's the rich who can afford the time necessary to make dedicated artworks, rather than having to spend all their time caring for the necessities of survival.

Similarly, because there now exists an 'upper class' who has at least some degree of leisure time, significant developments in mathematics, the sciences and technology are likely to occur in Stage 2. Accordingly, art is often centred on concepts of perfect mathematical and geometrical forms, as well as the mathematics of nature (think of Da Vinci's famous sketch of the proportions of man).

DID YOU KNOW?

Have you ever heard of the colour 'baby-poo yellow'? If you were living in the French courts in the late 1700s you would have! During this period, a highly fashionable (and very expensive) colour was caca dauphine—literally, the (baby) prince's poo. Wearing this colour was seen as an outward sign of support for the monarchy, and wealthy individuals might spend the equivalent of thousands of dollars on this charming fashion trend.

STAGE 3

- Declining birth rates
- Low death rates
- Industrialisation and mass-production
- Population growth starts out rapid and gradually slows throughout this stage
- Key threats: pollution, prejudicial violence (racial, gender, etc.), population growth

FOOD

In Stage 3, time-saving technology begins to play a role in food production. The increased (and still increasing, though more slowly than in Stage 2) population means that people are packed together ever more tightly, and there is physically less room for food production; this plus the technological advances seen in this stage means that a lot of food production and preparation is outsourced, both from individuals and from growing urban centers.

The importance of regularly bonding together over food consumption may begin to decrease now, as it's no longer necessary to devote large chunks of time to food preparation.

Families are likely to become smaller due to the declining birth rate, and time spent in the home is less common. Because of this, the cultural signif-

STAGE 3

icance of food on a day-to-day basis may begin to decline. Eating together becomes a 'special' event in some places, with festivals and celebrations that reinforce community, and may include an element of religiosity, rather than a daily occurrence.

More and more women will be able to access formal education in this stage, so they have less time to spend on food preparation. This can lead to an emphasis on the benefits of quickly-prepared food. This, combined with new food technologies, means that commercially-prepared food can become popular and 'fast food' develops from street stalls and markets to industrialised, synthetically (and thus cheaply) manufactured foods that emphasise *uniformity* as the key measure of quality assurance.

CLOTHING

The increase in industrialisation and mass-production means that it's now likely to be cheaper and more time effective to buy clothing rather than make it. This is also driven by the development of faster and more efficient transport, as clothes can be made cheaply in one area and transported relatively quickly to another.

These cloth-making and clothes-making factories have been historically staffed predominantly by women, particularly in societies that were plough-

STAGE 3

based and hence have institutionalised gender inequality (though the status of women has not been high in any society, really). This is because male access to education and paid work outside the home in Stage 2 means that by the time the population moves into Stage 3, women are already significantly disadvantaged in terms of job opportunities and so are the most easily available workforce to staff the burgeoning factories.

Tailor-made clothing is still popular and relatively common in this stage, but mass-market clothing steadily gains a larger and larger market share.

Trousers are likely to gradually become a valid

DID YOU KNOW?

Industrialisation relies on there being a market for the goods that are created, so when industrialisation occurred in western countries, there was a need to promote cotton and woollen clothes, the main bulk products of the time. This is why, in colonised countries, cotton and wool often replaced the traditional, locally-produced clothing, despite the fact that cotton and wool may be more difficult or more expensive for the local population to obtain. However, after the World Wars, the availability of cotton and wool fell due to post-war shortages. This, combined with new technology, made synthetic fabrics cheap and appealing.

STAGE 3

clothing choice for everyone in temperate to cool climates due to their practicality. The distinctions between "kid clothes" and "adult clothes" begin to diminish, as does (in some areas) the line between formal and informal clothing, in part because complex clothing is now so much easier to make.

(Consider: why would you make complex clothing for children, who will outgrow the item in less than a year, or wreck it before then, when you could dress them all alike in a simple shift- or robe-like garment? It just isn't financially feasible, or a good use of time until commercially-made clothing becomes a viable option.)

Synthetic fabrics gradually become available as technology develops, widening the options and flexibility of clothing generally (though remember that, due to globalisation and the influence of trade partners further down the demographic timeline, sometimes populations earlier on the timeline can also access synthetic clothing—see comments in Stage 2 clothing).

This is the stage in which fashion is likely to take off as an industry in its own right, made possible partly because there is now likely to be an increasingly-large middle class with disposable income to spend on numerous sets of clothes, and partly because mass-market clothing needs to be advertised, which means you need models to advertise it *on*.

STAGE 3

The theme here generally is ever-greater complexity: more complex designs, more complex materials, more complex fasteners (e.g. zippers, Velcro, etc), more complex designs on the actual fabric itself, and a wider (more complex!) range of colours, made possible due to the invention of synthetic dyes.

SHELTER

It's during Stage 3 that urban centres start to form, and as they do, they often separate into 'districts'. Sometimes this is a result of governmental intervention, but often any interventions come after or in reaction to the natural formation of districts that separate people by class, race, religion, or income potential.

In particular, there is a significant rise in 'shanty towns' and slums as people flock to the cities for work. Overcrowded rural areas can't support high rural populations any more (because the death rate is falling, remember, so the population size is still rising), and the expansion of industry and national/international trade means that employment in the cities is booming.

Often, in poorer countries, there *is* only a single dominant city, with a handful of medium-sized cities, so if people want work, that's where they have to do.

STAGE 3

Lower socioeconomic areas are likely to develop in areas that are physically less desirable: lower elevations, areas prone to flooding or bogginess, areas subject to pollution from either waterways or air (consider the prevailing winds and the way they will direct air pollutants), and so forth.

However, infrastructure generally improves, as does access to amenities, and the population as a whole slowly settles into a balance between people in the inner city and outer suburbs. Flats and apartments become commonplace, and block work (frequently bricks or cinderblocks made from concrete) becomes the dominant building style in many areas, particularly in industrial areas where buildings need to be fireproof.

It's at this point that the long-term environmental effects of industrialisation, and now urbanisation, are likely to start to make themselves known.

Industry is booming in many areas, and this can mean mass clearing of forests for farming, large-scale mining operations (often strip mines that destroy the land), and the use of vast quantities of water for industries like agriculture and fashion.

Urban environments not only create pollution (air, land and water) and degrade the immediate surrounds, they also influence weather patterns. Urban environments tend to use a lot of concrete (precursors to modern concrete have been used for centuries, including in Ancient Rome, where five-storey apartment buildings known as *insulae* were relatively common in place), which retains heat from the day and radiates it back at night-time. Various vehicles and industries also radiate heat, and as a result, urban environments are often noticeably warmer than their rural surrounds. This can impact not only temperature, but also rainfall patterns, especially if the city affects the humidity content of the surrounding air. Smog and air pollution can also 'seed' clouds and make rain more likely downwind—though this rain could be acidic if the smog or air pollution contained high levels or sulphur and/or nitrogen oxides (the smoke generated by burning coal, for example).

As electricity becomes more common, light pollution also becomes a problem, which, in addition to the city's noise pollution, disrupts the cycles and migration patterns of wildlife (bats, moths, birds, whales, etc.). It also results in lower species diversity for all types of animals—although *moderate* levels of urbanisation can have positive impacts on bird and plant diversity.

FAMILY AND MARRIAGE

Eventually, the realisation that death rates have declined seeps through the public awareness and people 'realise' that they no longer need to have large numbers of children to offset infant and child mortality.

It's important to note that the rate at which this cultural 'realisation' occurs is determined largely by globalisation: the more globalised the world is (which generally means there is a high percentage of Stage 4 or 5 populations around), the more quickly other populations move along the demographic timeline.

DID YOU KNOW?

Biodiversity is often mentioned as an important thing to preserve, but few lay people can actually articulate why. So: the reason biodiversity is important is because ecosystems are, fundamentally, *systems*—specifically, systems in which the overall output is greater than the sum of its parts. Just as reducing the human body too far means we miss the complex interplay between the components, so too an ecosystem is full of complex, interdependent relationships—and an ecosystem that lacks diversity lacks the ability to function effectively. Some predictions suggest that, with our current rate of species loss, the Earth will be ill-equipped to provide for any of the needs of humanity within as little as 100 years, with the effects of this loss of diversity being likened to a nuclear winter.

STAGE 3

The number of women in the workforce and/or in teen education increases; age of first marriage slowly begins to creep upwards (although the most significant jump occurs at the end of this stage when female education becomes widespread, since the longer you stay in school, the older you are when you get married, and the fewer children you end up having).

These factors, along with advances in both options for and the availability of contraceptive technology, all mean that birth rates begin to decline. This is also driven by the increasing urbanisation and the outsourcing of tasks that used to be done in the home, like food preparation and making clothes, which means that families have less need for so many extra hands around the house, and children start to cost more to raise than they are able to contribute to the economy of the household. However, the role of urbanisation in lowering the birth rate is more likely to affect people in 'high-quality' urban environments, meaning there is a distinctly classist aspect to this, with upper and middle class segments of the population lowering their birth rates faster than working class segments of the population, who are forced to live in poorer-quality areas.

Linked to this is the factor of access to education: education is likely to be widely recognised as a good thing now, something that results in

STAGE 3

access to employment, increased wealth, and increased status (knowledge is power, after all), and so compulsory schooling is usually introduced at this stage in a population's lifespan—although in cultures with a gender imbalance, boys are generally expected to attend school for longer than girls.

(This is also, tragically, the era of child exploitation, where five-year-olds may be sent out to work in factories and weaving mills, and sweatshops are often staffed by young girls. Note the complex political dynamics at play here, though: often, the labour done by these children is not necessarily for the benefit of their own society, but rather for the benefit of neighbouring Stage 4 or 5 populations.)

Education also adds to the cost of raising children, as does the increasing expectation that children need toys for entertainment (something that benefits the growing corporations, who are the ones to benefit most from the transition into Stage 3, and indicative of a newly-established belief in childhood as not only a discrete stage from adulthood, but one to be celebrated lavishly).

However, declining birth rates may also exacerbate already-established baby gender preferences. In cultures where a strong preference for male children has already taken firm hold, a declining fertility rate driven by a desire for smaller families and reduced costs is likely to increase female infant/foetus mortality overall, while simultaneously reducing male infant/foetus mortality.

In addition, most societies that we have seen on Earth have failed to equalise work done in the private sphere, even as they have admitted women into the public sphere; this means that, particularly in cultures where men have had only tokenistic roles in child rearing, women may end up with a double burden of responsibility in both the private and the public domains.

The decreasing birth rate and low death rate lead to an eventual ageing of the population toward the end of this stage.

In some societies, this results in attitudes towards elderly people become 'radicalised' in one direction or the other.

- The elderly might be seen as a burden on an already over-taxed society in cultures where human beings are valued for their earning potential;
- or else they might be viewed as an expanding pool of knowledge and intellectual resources in cultures where people are acknowledged as intrinsically valuable.

(It's worth considering too the flow-on effects of either of these perspectives; what impact would valuing earning potential versus human dignity

STAGE 3

have on a culture's style of eating, clothing manufacture, housing expectations, economic development, and so forth?)

The occurrence of multi-generational families begins to decline (which often encourages the trend of seeing old people as a burden), and in some cultures, elderly people begin to be segregated away from mainstream society.

Elderly parents live for longer and the gaps between generations increase, meaning that where once grandparents were likely to be in their thirties or forties when grandchildren were born, now they are likely to be in their fifties or sixties. This means that in gender-imbalanced cultures, women are now not only stepping out into the public sphere while maintaining the private sphere, they are also potentially caring for both children and elderly relatives (hence the appeal of sending elderly people to homes, and the shift towards seeing the elderly as a burden, something further reinforced by the move away from family-managed careers to corporate careers).

Conversely, though, as the stage progresses and more families become dual-wage families, there is also a significant return to grandparents doing a large portion of the child-minding (sometimes even rearing their grandchildren completely) as can be seen in earlier stages before the changes of early Stage 3.

STAGE 3

ECONOMIC DEVELOPMENT

I noted in the introduction to Part Two that birth and death rates rule supreme when determining a population's stage: although most people tend to assume that economic development and investment in infrastructure are what kicks a population over into Stage 3, it really is the falling death rate that defines the move from Stage 2 to Stage 3. It is only once mortality fall to a certain level that a drop in birth rates is triggered (although as ever, there are plenty of complicating factors). This is partly why it takes some populations longer to get to Stage 3 than others: all other factors being equal, if the population has a super high death rate to begin with, it will take much longer for it to reach that low mortality point than it will for populations which only had a moderate death rate in Stage 2.

In Stage 2 economics I noted that studies have conclusively demonstrated that some form of stable government is necessary for a population not to fail at Stage 2. This means that by the time the population gets to Stage 3, the government will be well entrenched. If they have been successful, they should have been investing in things like health and sanitation, water supply, medical centres, education, and infrastructure like roads, energy and communications technology, all of which will also improve the economic situation of

STAGE 3

the population. These in turn help to improve general health and knowledge, further lowering the death rate—and hopefully, a positive cycle begins.

Thus, Stage 3 is not so much about changes in government as it is about consolidating what's already in place—although if democracy is going to be introduced, this is when it's most likely to be successful.

In terms of economics, there are two main options at this point: a market-style system, or a command-style system. In practice, most populations end up with a murky combination of the two, but for simplicity's sake, a market system is one which is entirely unregulated (unlikely, given that government regulation is essentially a prerequisite to getting through Stage 2 successfully!), where vendors are entirely free to create/sell any products they desire, and customers are free to buy or not buy as they wish.

The theory behind this, which is the theory underpinning much of capitalism, is that the marketplace will regulate itself: consumers will naturally head towards products which represent best quality for least cost, and thus the companies providing these goods or services will be rewarded, while companies producing poor quality goods/services, or goods/services that are too pricey will be punished through lack of business.

STAGE 3

Although this is sound in theory, it very rarely works perfectly in practice; large corporations with financial backing are able to seduce the population through clever marketing strategies that are independent of the quality of the final product, and they have the ability to minimise their costs through mass production.

Small business, on the other hand, does not have the economic resources to mount glitzy marketing campaigns. They may compete by providing a higher quality product, particularly to niche markets, but this is only likely to be feasible until big-business competition emerges.

Command systems go the opposite extreme: *everything* is regulated. The advantage of such as system is that, theoretically, people are taken care of with free education, health and aged care, and so forth. Vendors are told by legislation from the government what they can and can't sell, produce or provide, and at what cost—and through similar legislation, buyers know what to expect.

While on the one hand this can protect against the 'buyer beware' vulnerabilities of a market system, it can be flawed in that it relies entirely on an uncorrupted government to function. The lack of private ownership and decision-making can also be a disincentive to productivity, since it doesn't really matter if you make more than your neighbour, because it's all going to be taken away by the government and redistributed anyway—so what's the point in working hard? Because of this, it's easy for such a society to stagnate.

In practice, as mentioned before, most economic systems are a blend of the two, though the population will usually lean towards one or the other, with the majority of economic systems in effect on Earth today being some variant of a mixed, market-based economy. Regardless, Stage 3 is the stage in which these practices are consolidated and codified.

HEALTH AND MEDICINE

Like many other areas of culture in this stage, medical knowledge becomes entwined with science. In a period where technology begins to advance exponentially, science, it seems, has the answers to everything.

Historically, this led to a reductionist approach to the human body: the body was compared to the ever-more-sophisticated machines that were being created and, like machines, was believed to be reducible to its component parts.

The effects of this reductionist thinking are threefold. First, medicine becomes interested in the minute functioning of illness, exploring disease on smaller and smaller levels, eventually searching for the answers to the question of illness

STAGE 3

at the cellular and subcellular level. This results in medicine becoming increasingly specialised, such that even a highly-trained medical practitioner cannot possibly know all the mechanics of the body outside of their specialisation—making medicine, therefore, increasingly inaccessible to the layperson.

Doctors become elevated because of the vast knowledge society presumes they must have, and the power/authority dynamics of the interaction between doctor and patient changes accordingly.

Secondly, reductionism leads to simplification, and therefore to more targeted strategies. Where once medicinal treatments might have involved broad application of generally effective treatments, now specialist knowledge makes specialist treatments available: this drug for that condition, that therapy for this condition, and so forth.

However, the danger of this is that disease becomes over-simplified. When disease or illness is reduced entirely to its component parts, there's no way to account for symptoms or phenomena that may be present and yet may not have an obvious cause at a cellular level. (An example of this is life itself, something that cannot be explained or defined simply in terms of an interaction between atoms, molecules, or even cells.)

This can result in drugs being promoted as 'magic bullet' cures without adequate regard for their side- or long-term effects—and indeed, health and illness in this period more so than any other is characterised by a series of popular fads and ever-cycling trends regarding both treatments and preventions such as vitamins, tonics and the like.

Thirdly, while reductionism seeks to answer questions surrounding illness, it often ends up creating more questions than it answers, particularly because it can lead to chicken-and-egg type situations: to know that a particular illness is always accompanied by a particular activity at the cellular level is one thing, but to know whether the cellular activity is the cause of the illness, or a symptom of the illness, is another thing entirely.

ART AND BEAUTY

In the third stage, urbanisation on top of industrialisation redefines society. This, in addition to all the technological advances going on, makes possible a whole range of cosmetics and pharmaceuticals that aren't available during prior stages.

In keeping with the positivity initially inspired by this technological boom, chemistry-based, scientifically-formulated products are equated with both cutting-edge health care—and beauty. Consequently, the commercial beauty industry explodes, especially in the later parts of Stage 3, with a product designed to cure every beauty ill—and, as technology advances, an improved ability to actually function as claimed.

This is also driven by the increasingly technical context in which 'beautiful people' are seen; better camera lenses, artificial lighting, the commonplaceness of mirrors and so forth, mean that flaws which were previously unimportant (such as the condition of the skin) now become extremely noticeable—and correcting them equally important. This is, of course, also facilitated by the fact that a larger segment of the population has money to spend on non-essentials: at this point in the

DID YOU KNOW?

In the western world, women's clothing didn't really reveal any hairy skin prior to Stage 3, so body hair was never an issue. But with the advent of sleeveless dresses in the west, razor manufacturers realised they could tap into a whole new segment of the market and began publishing instructional adverts designed to teach women how to shave 'unsightly' hair from all this newly-exposed skin—which gradually expanded in definition to include leg hair, and then as modest standards relaxed even further, pubic hair too—and thus was a lucrative segment of the beauty industry born.

STAGE 3

society's development, there is likely to be a distinct and booming middle class.

Fashion, too, begins to take greater risks, both because new materials and ways of constructing clothing are now possible, and because this sense of possibility inspired by technological and scientific advancement inspires a sense of risk-taking with regards to formerly-codified standards of behaviour, dress, modesty and so forth.

Additionally, since females are likely to be participating more in the public sphere in this

Did You Know?

Although historical clothing for women is often thought of as restrictive and highly conservative, in many places throughout history it was perfectly acceptable for a woman to flash a nipple because her dress was so low cut (witness the many formal portraits of women with bare or partially exposed breasts).

In fact, in parts of Europe prior to the Victorian era, aristocrats sometimes applied blue pencils to the breasts to increase the visibility of the veins, and the areola and nipple may have been rouged.

If a woman were to show a shoulder or an ankle, however... Gasp! Scandal!

(Incidentally, this is why table cloths, or table skirts, were invented, because heaven forbid anyone see the legs of the table and get ideas.)

stage (through both education and employment), female sexuality is likely to gradually become publicly acceptable (or at least *more* acceptable).

This also has a dramatic influence on fashion and standards of beauty. At the most basic level, this means that in cultures with stricter modesty codes, female skin will probably start to become less taboo.

Did You Know?

There is a general trend for populations to have darker skin in areas with intense sun exposure, such as the tropics (the extra melatonin helps protect against radiation damage), and lighter skin in areas with less intense sun exposure, such as cold temperate climates (allowing for quicker uptake of Vitamin D, maximising the sun exposure that is received). Estimates suggest that, controlling for all other variables (particularly immigration and subsequent marriage of people with different skin tones), it would take about a hundred generations for the genetically encoded skin colour of a population to 'drift' to match its environment.

However, this isn't always guaranteed. For example, on Earth, the native Alaskan people have very minimal solar radiation exposure, and yet do not have pale white skin—so like everything else, consider this a guideline only.

STAGE 3

Generally speaking, standards of beauty in this stage of the transition reflect well-established notions of health, youth and symmetry (as in all stages), but in nations following a western paradigm, the trend gradually begins to sway towards browner (tanned) skin rather than paler skin, as it becomes fashionable for rich people to have leisure time in the sun.

As blue-collar jobs migrate from the field to the factory because of industrialisation, so too desirable skin colour in these populations migrates from the parlour to the beach promenade. The lower working classes become paler as they are now working indoors, and so to continue to differentiate themselves, the upper classes seek to become sun-darkened as evidence of their ability to laze around in the sun, avoiding hard work.

Note that the terms 'paler' and 'darker' in this context apply within the bounds of each individual culture; what is considered 'pale' in one culture, may be considered 'dark' in another.

There are of course a lot of complicating factors here. First of all, the beauty standards from the previous era might have become so entrenched that they don't end up shifting here (this happened, for example, in China, in which paler skin has long been a component of beauty, even prior to extensive European contact).

Second of all, this shift relies on the population

having a skin tone that is actually responsive to sun exposure. In a population with very dark skin, for example, the skin tone of the upper class would not shift due to their sun exposure, and so skin tone would be less likely to be a component of their beauty standard (or if it is, it won't be because the rich can holiday in the sun, but will be for another reason).

And finally, it's important to consider the impact of the surrounding populations. If one population with a notably different skin tone is seen as dominant (either regionally or globally), then it's reasonably likely that their standards of beauty will colonise other populations.

So think things through carefully, and be aware of *why* your population is acting as it is.

Regardless of all this discussion about skin tone, due to the increased education of women and their subsequent participation in the public sphere, it's no longer fashionable for women to appear as frail and fainty as in the previous stage.

STAGE 4

- Low birth rate
- Low death rate
- Increasingly digital and globalised society
- Stable population size
- Key threats: over-consumption, environmental damage, energy production

FOOD

By the time a society reaches Stage 4, the whole chain of food production, preparation and consumption is largely in the hands of agri-business monopolies or giant multi-national corporations.

Food consumption is often fitted in around other commitments, and technological advances allow for 'meal supplements' or 'meal replacements' and pre-packaged dinners, as well as extended shelf lives for the vast majority of foods. Supermarkets are a standardised and expected part of the food landscape.

However, this is also the stage where the concept of 'food deserts' emerges: urbanised areas that do not have any direct access to food, both through a lack of adequate grocery stores and through the inability to produce one's own food due to the urban environment. Usually, these food deserts are correlated with lower socioeconomic

STAGE 4

areas and lead to a host of health problems, stemming from the fact that nutritious, high-quality and high-taste foods are hard to come by, and so-called 'empty' calories are cheaper and more plentiful.

Concurrent with this, advances in health science begin to reveal that corporate food is not always as nutritious as originally thought. Because of this, later Stage 4 societies may see a resurgence of interest in the food production/preparation/consumption triad, with segments of the population beginning to reject corporate control of their food. Localised markets may become popular again; home gardens become fashionable in some demographics; and the organic market is born (often correlating to a rise in concern for the state

Did You Know?

Contemporary research suggests that nutrition and taste are actually tightly linked: vegetables with higher nutritional qualities taste better than their less-nutritious counterparts.

This isn't a discussion of kale versus grapes; rather, well-grown, nutrient-packed grapes taste better than grapes with a poor nutritional profile. To our bodies, it seems that taste and nutrition are actually one and the same.

STAGE 4

of the planet, with widespread ecosystem degradation having resulted from earlier-stage agricultural practices). However—as ever—the higher socioeconomic groups are more likely to have access to this 'better' food, while the lower socioeconomic demographics may continue to favour the commercially prepared food which is, somewhat ironically, often more cost effective than less processed foods, especially since space in urban environments is at a premium.

CLOTHING

Apart from minor segments of the population who swing back to 'traditional' ways of doing things, clothing is likely to be manufactured en masse and sold commercially. The technology behind synthetic fabrics develops further, and clothing can be wrinkle-free, wicking, insulating, fast-drying, stain-resistant, water-resistant, and a whole host of other features previously unimaged.

Dress standards differ wildly not only between nations, but also within, though there are still likely to be 'dress-codes' stipulating when it is appropriate to wear each type of clothing (and also the appropriate degree of skin one may show)—although as globalisation continues, boundaries begin to break down and individual preference becomes an important factor.

STAGE 4

The emphasis is on a wide variety of options, with hundreds of fabric types and synthetic dyes capable of replicating any imaginable colour. The styles and designs of available clothing are, however, driven by the fashion industry, now likely to be a multi-billion dollar industry that seeks to elevate clothing to an art form.

In the later parts of this stage, awareness of factory conditions and labour exploitation (often of populations in earlier stages of the demographic transition) is likely to develop, and clothing choices split down two channels: on one hand, clothing is available more cheaply than ever before due to cheap, usually off-shore manufacturing.

On the other hand, 'ethical clothing' companies may begin to appear that at least claim to treat and pay their workers fairly; buying an item of clothing is no longer a personal, private matter, but a public consumption and human rights decision (note the ever-increasing movement of clothing from the private to the public sphere).

As part of the counter-culture movement away from commercialism and industrialism, many cultures may be drawn to reclaim their native dress, or combine their historical modes of dress with modern technology to recreate their sense of cultural identity. This trend even begins to permeate Big Fashion, with haute couture beginning to celebrate designers from around the world as

STAGE 4

populations reach Stage 4 and globalisation increases.

SHELTER

As urban centres grow, sustainable housing becomes a concern. Environmentally speaking, urban developments can actually be *more* sustainable than rural living for large populations if they're done right. Not only would we soon run out of land if every nuclear family needed several acres each to live on (especially since the lands that are desirable are the fertile bits, which should ideally be saved for food production and grazing), but governments can provide services such as water and sanitation and electricity more cost-effectively to denser populations.

However, since corporations are likely to be in control of the economy at this point, sustainability is often sacrificed for profit margins, with housing being made ever more cheaply, and the design and construction thereof being out-sourced to yet more corporations; in many ways, the developments of Stage 4 are about supporting the proliferation of the corporation.

Technological advances made in other areas are incorporated into housing, including: superior insulation; more efficient heating and cooling systems; alternate energy sources such as solar panels; rain water tanks; and a variety of other features designed to reduce the amount of energy and water a house uses.

Commercial and residential buildings diverge significantly in terms of building materials, form, and location, with glass-steel-concrete constructions becoming first possible due to the improved technology, and then common for commercial buildings.

In later parts of this stage, prefabricated housing may become an option; project housing companies might be established where people can 'buy off the plan', and as mass consumerism dominates the population, so too do mass-designed and/or produced houses—though as with many other areas, counter-cultures arise that value architect-designed buildings, enviro-designs and sustainable development, with many decrying the homogenisation of skyscrapers and urban housing developments as the stage progresses.

FAMILY AND MARRIAGE

In this stage, deaths are low due to increased knowledge about both medicine and hygiene, and it's possible to not only preserve life, but to extend it. Rates of childbirth are also low, largely due to the ability to choose and plan families; women's

STAGE 4

increased role in the public domain; and the increased cost of raising children, due to a pervasive belief in the importance of formal education.

By now, at least in predominantly market-based cultures, consumerism is also likely to have kicked in as the dominant ideology unless specific steps were taken at earlier stages that counteract this—further increasing the cost of child raising as corporations seek to promote toys, electronic devices, clothing and food all designed for children's consumption.

(This is also where gender stereotypes tend to be drawn down to apply to younger and younger children; it suits the corporations for toys to be gendered—an incomprehensible luxury in earlier stages—because that way, if you have children of different genders, you have to rebuy all your products—a blue pram instead of a pink one, new bedding, new room décor, etc.)

Further into mid Stage 4, families may no longer be nuclear. Increased female participation in the public sphere leads to increased political rights for women in societies where significant gender gaps exist (recall that whether or not significant, systemically-entrenched gender gaps exist is often due to the choice between plough agriculture and shifting agriculture, discussed in Stage 1), and options regarding divorce and abortion are likely to gain wider acceptance.

STAGE 4

Thus, families diversify: some may remain multi-generational, some may consist of parents and children, and some may consist of members of the same generation sharing space together. Single parents, single people, and single children all become normalised.

In general, looking after children and the elderly (particularly the elderly) shifts towards the public sphere, following the trend of women's work, food production, clothing manufacture, and so forth: institutions are established to care for both children (during work hours so that women may work) and the elderly (again, at least initially, so that women may work).

It is worth noting that at this stage, as in Stage 1, a population can remain stable for many decades, if not centuries, in the absence of external factors (such as wars, natural disasters, etc.).

ECONOMIC DEVELOPMENT

Whereas in Stage 3 industrialisation and urbanisation are the buzzwords, in Stage 4 the buzzword is digitisation. As technology increases, 'virtual money' becomes the prevailing form of currency. Rather than exchanging product for product (barter economies), or exchanging precious metals for product (basic currency economies), or even the tangible promise of precious metals for product

STAGE 4

(currency economies that use bank notes), in digitised cultures, it becomes commonplace to exchange a digital number for a tangible product.

This requires a significant shift in cultural thinking, as well as an implicit level of trust in technology from society—which is why it's only possible in Stage 4, once technological advances have become sufficiently entrenched in society so as to engender mostly-unquestioning trust.

Think about it: in what other scenario could someone offer you something entirely unreal and imaginary for a physical, tangible product? Certainly, the recipient of the digital sum has the possibility of drawing this money physically out of a bank (though fewer and fewer people tend to as such technologies increase, instead simply shifting around intangible numbers in equally intangible 'accounts'), but it's a well-known fact that were everyone to suddenly decide that they wanted to convert all their digital, pretend sums into real, physical cash, no bank would be able to provide it all. There simply isn't enough physical money there backing it all.

Correspondingly, this shift not only shows an implicit trust in technology, but also values highly conceptual thinking.

Society shifts from being a product-based culture to an ideas-based culture (not unrelated to the fact that education is now widespread and mostly accessible), where knowledge—always a currency of its own—becomes widely recognised as not just as *a*, but *the* ultimate source of power.

Linked to this, an increasing demand for education drives the economy: in 2010, for example, education was Australia's second most financially significant 'export', as overseas students flocked to its universities.

Also as a consequence of the shift from product-based to concept-based, and facilitated by new (global) technologies, digital products in general become more common, and ideas themselves become valuable commodities that may be commercialised and sold.

The rise of virtual products, online banking, and online shopping changes the marketplace; consumers have access to products and services well beyond their usual reach, potentially from all over the globe, from populations at nearly any stage of technological development. In a market-based population, the market becomes even more buyer-driven as technology provides ways for people to share reviews, make recommendations, search out information, and have tangible products delivered straight to their door.

In a command economy, regulations must become tighter and more restrictive as technology opens up loopholes and ways around the already-existing regulations.

STAGE 4

Advertising remains, as ever, an integral part of this process—although many studies show that word of mouth still beats everything else when it comes to consumer decisions generally—and big companies are further able to outsource their labour as communications technology facilitates quick turnarounds and efficient long-distance communication.

Later in the stage, physical retailers may begin to disappear, particularly in mid-level luxury industries such as music and publishing. This is because as globalisation increases, technology allows consumers to reconnect with the producers themselves rather than the middlemen, and this becomes more and more normalised in a 'gig economy'. This tangentially feeds the move back to artisan-style living in industries such as food and the arts, and is all facilitated by digital economies, which allow direct payment to creators and producers in far-distant locations around the globe.

HEALTH AND MEDICINE

Medical advances in the fourth stage continue to be driven both by technological developments and increased urbanisation.

Importantly, globalisation allows access to societies at other stages along the demographic

STAGE 4

transition timeline, creating a melting pot of ideas and a return to earlier, more holistic ways of understanding health and disease than were evident in Stage 3. Thus, so-called 'alternative treatments' such as acupuncture, osteopathy, energy manipulation, naturopathy, and cognitive therapy become increasingly more available and more popular.

This is at least in part because more technologically advanced societies tend to fetishise less technological societies' practices as 'more authentic', which can lead to the adoption of practices that are sometimes completely ineffectual, or even harmful, because of an invested belief in the importance of doing things the 'natural' way. It can also lead to cultural appropriation, or the taking of culturally significant objects or practices and subsequently using them in ways that strip them entirely of their cultural (and often spiritual) significance and, in the case of health practices, often stripping them of their efficacy as well.

Additionally, the increase in technology makes even specialist information accessible to significant proportions of the population, and while the dialogue between patient and health care professional is certainly not as open as in Stages 1 or 2, patients have the ability to become more informed about their options. This give them the ability to express preferences for certain types of treatment

STAGE 4

over others by 'shopping' at different healthcare facilities, or seeking out specialists whose health philosophies match their own.

The changes in lifestyle that accompany the transition to Stage 4 result in a change of focus for the healthcare profession. Infant mortality is no longer a pressing issue—though it obviously remains a significant and meaningful topic—and instead much more attention is given to 'old age' diseases. Chronic diseases also become increasingly common because of the Stage 4 lifestyle—characteristically one of less physical exertion and poorer nutritional choices, combined with more-than-adequate calorie intake.

As the stage progresses, knowledge and awareness about these 'lifestyle diseases' increase in the general population, and a level of expectation

Did You Know?

We often attribute poor diet and the subsequent poor nutrition with so-called 'food deserts', or urban areas with very limited access to high-quality fresh foods. However, research suggests that 'urban swamps' are actually a better predictor of obesity and a host of diet-related health concerns. An 'urban swamp' is an area with a high density of fast-food outlets, selling high-calorie, low-nutrition convenience food.

STAGE 4

develops that people will take active steps to preserve their health.

To fully understand the impact of this, imagine explaining the purpose of a gym to someone in a Stage 1 or 2 population; the classic line from the classic film trilogy, *Back To The Future*, sums it up rather succinctly: "People *run* for *fun?*"

'Work-life balance' becomes both a common and necessary concept; mental illnesses become both more widely recognised and more effectively treatable, as well as more common due to higher-stress work environments and the psychological demands of a global society; and information about environmental concerns and sustainability (particularly regarding pollutants) becomes influential.

ART AND BEAUTY

This stage is much like the outcome of chaos theory: tiny changes in the earlier stages can result in large difference at this later stage.

While some standards of beauty have a biological impetus (youth means a greater likelihood of health and fertility; clear skin signals health; symmetry signals physical prowess; full, red lips are attractive because that's where blood naturally gathers during sexual attraction and activity;

STAGE 4

candlelight is romantic because it induces dilation of the pupils, mimicking their dilation during sex; etc.), some are driven by influences in society that much of the population are unaware of.

For example, many scholars attribute the rise in popularity in western culture of very large breasts to the pornography industry, where big boobs are preferred for legal reasons, quite aside from any aesthetic—small breasts verge too close to being childlike, and in striving as hard as possible to avoid associations with child pornography, the preferred breast size in pornographic images is 'as large as possible'.

Likewise, the trend for hairless pubic areas also started with pornography in the 1990s, partially as a bid to reveal yet more skin (although as of writing, this trend seems to be following the counter-culture swing back to everything *au naturel*, with big celebrity names recently speaking out in favour of the more natural look) and partially to make things more, uh, visible.

The skinny archetype currently in fashion in most western nations can be traced to the rise in popularity of a single model in the 1960s named Twiggy, who fought against tremendous self-esteem issues growing up because she was considered far too thin and almost entirely unattractive compared to the prevailing standards of beauty at the time.

STAGE 4

Her success as a model, however, inverted the western ideal of beauty entirely, and extreme thinness became fashionable because designers liked the more 'neutral' frame her thin body provided for displaying their clothing—and a generically 'thin' body is much easier to design clothing for than bodies which vary greatly in their individual proportions.

Probably, this was supported by the population's evolving relationship with food, as well; as nutrients became ever more readily available, and as 'junk' food became cheaper than fresh food, obesity became an epidemic, especially in poor or working-class areas where people couldn't afford to eat nutritious, high-quality food.

Once again, the upper classes were forced to adapt their standards of beauty in order to differentiate them-selves: *they* were not the lower class citizens who toiled away to consume vast quantities of empty calories; rather they were the privileged few who could afford the increasingly expensive fresh food, along with gym memberships, personal trainers, dieticians and the like to coach them to perfect health and fitness.

This also reflects the fact that the increasing application of technology to clothing and fashion resulted in a shift away from clothing determining a woman's figure for her. The emphasis shifted to controlling the body from the inside, rather than

STAGE 4

mechanically from the outside.

Thus the transformation of beauty standards in western, Earthly nations.

For your own culture, consider carefully how increased technology is going to interact with your population's class structure, and think about what your rich people are going to do to differentiate themselves from the rest of the population.

But also remember that despite this underlying and consistent trend throughout history for standards of beauty to reflect the lifestyle of the rich and popular, by the time a population reaches Stage 4, it's likely to have fairly extensive contact with many other populations.

Even early in this stage, education, travel technology and communications are sufficiently developed for the first truly globalising forces to make themselves felt. These lead to a subtle, gradual, but nonetheless influential and important cultural realisation that there are more valid perspectives in the world than just one.

Post-colonialism allows value to be placed on diversity; cultural ideologies are deconstructed, and "truth" becomes in many ways mutable and personal.

The varied experience of the individual becomes not only valid but valued, and this is reflected in groundswell campaigns seeking to level the beauty playing field.

STAGE 4

These general sentiments are tied together in the philosophy of post-modernism, a philosophy directly born from this increased global contact: one of its key characteristics is seeking to deconstruct standards of all kinds. Tradition is no longer a good enough reason to do anything, and the motive behind standards, particularly with reference to subtle power plays and systemic privilege, becomes a more important factor.

Recognition that established systems favour certain types of people over others develops (see the philosophy of Structuralism), and these systems and the standards they set (of dress, of beauty, of manner, of language, of behaviour) are systematically deconstructed.

Of course, the natural response to this by the people currently favoured by or profiting from these establish systems is defensive. Because of this, we see the development of a population in which, paradoxically, public support for the deconstruction of oppressive standards has never been higher, but public buy-in to *support* these same oppressive standards has also never been higher.

(There are more campaigns extant now than ever before reminding people that they should 'love the skin they're in', but modern western society is also characterised at the same time by a greater-than-ever-before preoccupation with un-

STAGE 4

realistic beauty standards—especially with regards to female beauty, although it has certainly taken hold with the male population as well—and the need to conform to society's increasingly-oppressive standards.)

RELIGION

A NOTE ON RELIGION

Discussing religion by demographic stage is nigh impossible: religions arise as a factor of their environment as much as populations do, but making generalisations about them across demographic stages is trickier than for other cultural areas. And worse, it is counterproductive: religion's power is not in its conformity to the stages of the demographic timeline, but rather in its ability to transcend them.

Never underestimate the power of religion to shape a culture. Every other factor discussed so far can apply to a particular population, and yet they might exhibit characteristics entirely opposite of what would be expected—and the culprit is usually religion.

Belief in *something* is fundamental to the human psyche; we seek stories, explanations, meaning, in not only our own personal experiences, but in the nature of the cosmos.

In fact, in his ground-breaking research into the psychology of happiness, Martin Seligman suggested that a sense of meaning and purpose is not only desirable, it is fundamental to human well-being. And despite the often-vigorous battle between religion and science, the two ultimately

RELIGION

stem from the same root: the need for understanding.

But the relationship between religion and the demographic transition is particularly tangled because, as noted, religion tends to transcend demographic trends rather than conforming to them. This is largely due to religion's ability to exert a high level of influence over a population's birth rate.

In fact, lots of research into the exact relationship between fertility and religion has been conducted, with the results suggesting that if three conditions are present, religion will be the factor that determines the fertility rate of the population, rather than anything else.

These three conditions are that:

1) The religion actually says something about behaviours that impact fertility (a religion that had nothing to do with sexual relationships, for example, would be largely unable to influence fertility);

2) The religion has the ability to both communicate these values to its believers and to enforce them in some way (some sort of organisational hierarchy, and the threat of either earthly or after-worldly consequences for failing to conform);

3) The religion is central to its followers' identity, something they value or willingly conform to.

RELIGION

If these three conditions are met, then it is entirely possible for a population to defy all of the tendencies and 'guidelines' of the demographic transition timeline, particularly with regards to fertility (usually by keeping the fertility levels higher than they would otherwise be for the stage the population is at).

In the most general of terms, however, it is fair to say that religion plays a more important role in societies earlier on the demographic transition timeline. Studies have shown that, accounting for other variables, highly religious societies (or segments of society) tend to have higher birth rates than highly secular ones, and conversely, that national wealth and democratic, widespread access to education both tend to advance secularism.

CONCLUSION

So, there you have it: the multitude of ways in which a culture's geographical environment and technological capabilities will impact its development.

Never again will you have to play mix-and-match to create a culture, and your readers will stand in awe of your tremendous, plausibly-constructed societies.

Congratulations!

You're practically a geographer!

Of course, there's always more to learn. It's not just humans who are impacted by their environment—plants and animals are too! Watch out for *How To Create Life* (another *Inkprint Writers* title) to learn about all the various ways that plants and animals adapt to their environments, so that you can populate your worlds with realistic critters—and create your own spectacular lifeforms that sit naturally within their biomes.

Then, of course, there are all the ways in which your planet's landforms influence its weather, and how its weather patterns then determine its biomes!

If you'd like to learn how to create your own maps with accuracy and aplomb, then watch out for *How To Map* (*Inkprint Writers #5*), a comprehensive and easy-to-follow guide to creating a

CONCLUSION

gorgeous, plausible world for your populations to live in—and how to figure out where the different biomes are in the first place!

Thanks for joining me on this journey. I'd love to hear from you about your own experiences creating cultures.

I'm easy to find; you're most likely to get a response on Twitter (@ByAmyLaurens), but you can also hunt me down at www.amylaurens.com.

See you around!

ABOUT THE AUTHOR

AS WELL AS being an author of many non-fiction and fantasy titles, Amy Laurens is a qualified high school geography teacher. She studied demographic anthropology as part of her Masters degree, and has had a life-long interest in climate and geography, passing the geographical/meteorological theory component of her private pilot's licence at age fifteen!

Sadly, she never ended up taking to the skies—except in her imagination, where she enjoys speculating about all the ways that climate and the environment affect the development of human culture.

Amy has also published numerous other books, including the *Sanctuary* series of portal fantasy novels for children and the *Kaditeos* series of satirical fantasy for adults, some more non-fiction for writers (including the popular *How To Theme*), some non-fiction for people who are alive (mostly about dogs and parties, though not parties *with* dogs (yet?)), and a bunch of short stories.

You can find them all at:
www.amylaurens.com/books

COMING SOON!

Watch out for these other titles in the Inkprint Writers series, coming in 2019.

How To Create Life: Invent Plant And Animal Species That Really Fit Your World, A Reference For Writers, Gamers And Amateur Geographers!

How To Map: Be Accurate And Add Conflict To Your Story, A Reference For Writers, Gamers And Amateur Geographers!

SUPPORTERS

With additional thanks to my amazing Patreon supporters, Clare, Thea and Bethy <3

Sign up for as little as $1/month to receive monthly exclusive short stories, weekly writing updates, and more!

https://www.patreon.com/amylaurens

FREE EBOOK

Thank you for buying this book!

When you buy an Inkprint Press book in print, we like to thank you by offering you the ebook for free. Please head to:

http://www.inkprintpress.com/amy-laurens/how-to-create-cultures/

and use the coupon CULTURE100 to download your free copy in both .mobi and .epub formats. (The coupon will only work once.)

REFERENCES

PART ONE

Alexander, B., and Alexander, C. (2009). *Arctic Photo.* http://www.arcticphoto.com/index.asp

Australian and New Zealand Solar Energy Society. (n.d.) *Hot Humid House Design Considerations (Tropical).* Retrieved from: http:// www.anzses.org

Australian Museum. (n.d.). *Wild Kids – Animals of Woodland Habitats.* Retrieved from: https://australianmuseum.net.au/wild-kids-animals-of-woodland-habitats

Avataq Cultural Institute. (n.d.). "Illnesses." *Nunavimmiuts.* Retrieved from: http://www.avataq.qc.ca/en/Nunavimmiuts/Traditional-Medicine/ Illnesses/

Baer, L.A. (1996). "Boreal Forest Dwellers: The Saami in Sweden." *Unasylva: An International Journal of Forest and Forest Industries.* 47(3).

Biomes Group, Biology 1B Class. (2004). *The World's Biomes.* University of California Museum of Paleontology. Retrieved from: http://www.ucmp.berkeley.edu/exhibits/biomes/index.php

Chapagain, A. K.; Hoekstra, A. Y.; Savenije, H. H. G.; and Gautam, R. (2006). "The water footprint of cotton consumption: An assessment of the impact of worldwide consumption of cotton products on the water resources in the cotton producing countries." *Ecological Economics.* 60:186–203.

Clemings, R. (1996). *Mirage: the false promise of desert agriculture.* Random House: USA.

Common Aquatic Plants. (2010). Aquarius Systems: About. Retrieved from: http://www.aquarius-systems.com/

Conservation of Artic Flora and Fauna. (2013). "Chapter 5: Amphibians and Reptiles." *Arctic Biodiversity Assessment: 2013*. Arctic Council: Iceland.

Countries and Their Cultures. (n.d.) *World Culture Encyclopedia*. Retrieved from: http://www.everyculture.com.

CrisisTimes. (2015.) "Finding Food In The Desert." *CrisisTimes*. Retrieved from: http://crisistimes.com/

Curriculum Research & Development Group (CRDG), College of Education, University of Hawaii. (n.d.). "Weird Science: Types of Salts in Seawater." *Exploring Our Fluid Earth*. Retrieved from: https://manoa.hawaii.edu/exploringourfluidearth/chemical/chemistry-and-seawater/salty-sea/weird-science-types-salts-seawater

Davis, Emma Lou. (1963). "The Desert Culture of the Western Great Basin: A Lifeway of Seasonal Transhumance." *American Antiquity*. 29(20):202-212. DOI: 10.2307/278490

Easterling, W.E.; Aggarwal, P.K.; Batima, P.; et al. (2007). "Food, fibre and forest products." In Solomon, S.; Qin, D.; Manning, M.; et. al. (eds.), *Climate Change 2007: The Physical Science Basis. Contribution of Working Group I to the Fourth Assessment Report of the Intergovernmental Panel on Climate Change*. Cambridge University Press: UK. Pp 273–313.

Faculty of Natural Resource Management, Lakehead University. (n.d). "Boreal Forests of the World." *Boreal Forest*. Retrieved from: www. borealforest.org.

Food and Agriculture Organisation of the United Nations. (1995). "Historical Role of Palms In Human Culture". *Non-Wood Forest Products 10*. Retrieved from: http://www.fao.org/docrep/ x0451e/X0451e00.htm

Food and Agriculture Organisation of the United Nations. (2017). *FAOStat: Food and Agriculture Data*.

Retrieved from: http://www.fao.org/faostat/en/#home

Gadsby, Patricia. (2004). "The Inuit Paradox." *Discover Magazine.* October. Retrieved from: http://discovermagazine.com/2004/oct/inuit-paradox

Gobi Desert. (2010). Retrieved from: gobidesert.org

Goldi Productions. (2007). "The Plains People." *Canada's First Peoples.* Retrieved from: http://firstpeoplesofcanada.com/fp_groups/fp_plains5.html

Harris, Jessica B. (1998). *The Africa Cookbook: Tastes of a Continent.* Simon & Schuster: New York.

Heritage Community Foundation. (2005). "The People of the Boreal Forest." *Alberta Online Encyclopedia.* Retrieved from: http://www.albertasource.ca/boreal/ index.html

Huckell, Lisa W. (1993). "Plant Remains from the Pinaleño Cotton Cache, Arizona." *Kiva, the Journal of Southwest Anthropology and History.* 59 (2): 147–203.

Kids Do Ecology. (2004). "Estuaries." *World Biomes.* Retrieved from http://kids.nceas.ucsb.edu/biomes/index.html

Kroeber, A.L. (1976). *Handbook of the Indians of California.* Dover Publications: New York.

Kuensting. (n.d.). "NW Coniferous Forest Information." *SLUH BioWeb.* Retrieved from: http://www2.sluh.org/bioweb/nh/biomes/nwconiferousforest/index.html

Marasco, Ramona; Rolli, Eleonora; Ettoumi, Besma; et. al. (2012). "A Drought Resistance-Promoting Microbiome Is Selected By Root System Under Desert Farming." *PLOS One.* 7(1):1-14.

Marietta College Department of Biology and Environmental Science. (n.d.). *Biomes of the World.* http://w3.marietta.edu/~biol/biomes/biomes.htm

Maxwell, Robyn J. (2003). *Textiles of Southeast Asia: tradition, trade and transformation* (revised ed.). Tuttle

Publishing: USA.

McCann, James C. (2009). *Stirring the Pot: A History of African Cuisine*. Ohio University Press: USA.

Moorcroft, Paul R. (2007). "Unit 4: Ecosystems". *The Habitable Planet: A Systems Approach To Environmental Science*. Annenberg Foundation. Retrieved from: http://www.learner. org/courses/envsci/index.html

Native Art In Canada. (2006). "Woodland Indians." Retrieved from: http://www.native-art-in-canada.com/

Neufeld, J.D., and Mohn, W.W. (2005). "Unexpectedly high bacterial diversity in arctic tundra relative to boreal forest soils, revealed by serial analysis of ribosomal sequence tags." *Applied and Environmental Microbiology*, 71. 10: 5710-5718.

Offwell Woodland and Wildlife Trust. (1998). "Woodland Structure." *An Introduction to British Woodlands and Their Management*. Retrieved from: http://www.countrysideinfo.co.uk/woodland_manage/struct.htm

Osseo-Asare, F. (2005). "Food Culture in Sub-Saharan Africa." *Food culture around the world*. Greenwood Press.

Pearson Education. (2000). *The Major Biomes*. WGBH Educational Foundation: USA.

Pritzker, Barry M. (2000). *A Native American Encyclopedia: History, Culture, and Peoples*. Oxford University Press: UK.

Roche, Julian. (1994). *The International Cotton Trade*. Woodhead Publishing Ltd: England.

Sachs, J. D. (2001). "Tropical Underdevelopment." *NBER Working Paper* No. 8119. DOI: 10.3386/w8119.

Schaffner, Brynn. (2010). *Blue Planet Biomes*. Retrieved from http://www.blueplanetbiomes.org

Shkolnik, Amiram; Taylor, C. Richard; Finch, Virginia; and Borut, Arieh. (1980). "Why Do Bedouins Wear Black Robes in Hot Deserts?" *Nature*. 283:373-375.

Sholtz, Paul; Bretz, Michael; and Nori, Franco. (1997). "Sound-producing Sand Avalanches." *Contemporary Physics* 38(5). DOI: 10.1080/001075 197182306.

Slezak, Michael. (2014). "Pacific Coral Happy As Water Acidity Rises." *New Scientist* 2950, 4 Jan 2014.

Smith, Chuck. (2002). "Agricultural Societies In Pre-European Times: Southwestern U.S. and Northwestern Mexico." *Native Peoples of North America*. Retrieved from: http://www.cabrillo.edu/~crsmith/southwest.html

Stager, Lawrence E. (1976). "Farming in the Judean Desert During the Iron Age." *Bulletin of the American Schools of Oriental Research*. 221(Memorial Issue):145-158. DOI: 10.2307/ 1356097.

Stein, Burton. (1998). *A History of India*. Blackwell Publishing: USA.

Strutin, Michal. (1999). *A Guide to Contemporary Plains Indians*. Southwest Parks and Monuments Association: USA.

Thalmann, O.; Shapiro, B.; Cui, P.; et. al. (2013). "Complete Mitochondrial Genomes of Ancient Canids Suggest a European Origin of Domestic Dogs." *Science*. 342(6160):871-4. DOI: 10.1126/ science.1243650.

Tropical Dry Forests. (n.d.). Ceiba.org. Retrieved from: http://ceiba. org/conservation/dry-forests/

Tyman, John. (2014). *Inuit—People of the Arctic*. Pitt Rivers Museum, Oxford University. Retrieved from: http://www.johntyman.com/arctic/

Uprety, Yadav.; Asselin, Hugo; Dhakal, Archana; and Julien, Nancy. (2012). "Traditional Use of Medicinal Plants in the Boreal Forest of Canada: Review and Perspectives." *Journal of Ethnobiology and Ethnomedicine*. 8:7. DOI: 10.1186/1746-4269-8-7.

Veit, Veronika (2007). The Role of Women in the Altaic World. *Permanent International Altaistic Conference,*

44th Meeting, Walberberg, 26-31 August 2001. Harrassowitz Verlag: Germany.

Waness, Abdelkarim; El-Sameed, Yaser Abu; Mahboub, Bassam et. al. (2011). "Respiratory disorders in the Middle East: A review." *Respirology* 16(5):755 DOI: 10.1111/j.1440-1843.2011.01988.x.

Webb, Sam. (2013). "Tuberculosis 'Originated Among Human 70,000 Years Ago and Does Not Come From Animals'." *Daily Mail.* Retrieved from: https://www.dailymail.co.uk/health/article-2409120/Tuberculosis-originated-human-70-000-years-ago-does-NOT-come-animals.html

Woodward, Susan L. (1997). "Temperate Grasslands." *Biomes of the World.* Department of Geospatial Science, Radford University. Retrieved from: https://php.radford.edu/~swoodwar/biomes/?page_id=173

Woodward, Susan L. (1997). "Tropical Savannahs." *Biomes of the World.* Department of Geospatial Science, Radford University. Retrieved from: https://php.radford.edu/~swoodwar/biomes/?page_id=105

Woodward, Susan L. (2012). "Coral Reefs." *Biomes of the World.* Department of Geospatial Science, Radford University. Retrieved from https://php.radford.edu/~swoodwar/biomes/?page_id=837

Yabe, Mitsuo. (2003). "Trees and Forests, Part of the Cultural Fabric of Japan." *Nipponia.* 24(Mar). Retrieved from: https://web-japan.org/nipponia/nipponia24/en/

PART TWO

Alesino, Alberto; Giuliano, Paola; and Nunn, Nathan. (2013). "Traditional Farming Practices and the Evolution of Gender Norms Across the Globe." *OUP Blog*. Retrieved from: https://blog.oup.com/2013/06/agriculture-gender-roles-norms-society/

Bache, Ella. (n.d.). "The History of Beauty: History of Hair." *UK Hairdressers*. Retrieved from: https://www.ukhairdressers.com/history%20of%20beauty.asp

Barber, Dan. (2014). *The Third Plate: Field Notes on the Future of Food*. Penguin Books: USA.

Beresford, Mark J. (2010). "Medical Reductionism: Lessons From the Great Philosophers." *QJM: An International Journal of Medicine*. 103(9):721-4.

Blankenship, L. (2011). "Worldbuilding: Pre-industrial Medicine." *Notes From the Jovian Frontier*. Retrieved from: http://lblankenship.blogspot.com/2011/11/worldbuilding-pre-industrial-medicine.html

Bloom, David E.; Canning, David; and Sevilla, Jaypee. (2001). "Economic Growth and the Demographic Transition." *NBER Working Paper No. 8685*. DOI: 10.3386/w8685

Blume, Michael; Ramsel, Carsten; and Graupner, Sven. (2006). "Religiousity as a demographic factor—an underestimated connection?" *Marburg Journal of Religion*. 11(1).

Burnette, Joyce. (2008). "Women Workers in the British Industrial Revolution." *EH.net Encyclopedia*. Retrieved from: http://eh.net/encyclopedia/women-workers-in-the-british-industrial-revolution/

Cervellati, Matteo and Sunde, Uwe. (2008). "The Economic and Demographic Transition, Mortality and Comparative Development." University of St. Gallen,

Department of Economics, Discussion Paper No. 2008-21. Retrieved from: http://sticerd.lse.ac.uk/seminarpapers/dg17112008.pdf

Cohen, Barney. (2015). "Urbanization, City Growth, and the New United Nations Development Agenda." *Cornerstone: The Official Journal of the World Coal Industry.* 3(2):4-7.

Cooksey-Stowers, Kristen; Schwartz, Marlene B.; and Brownell, Kelly D. (2017). "Food Swamps Predict Obesity Rates Better Than Food Deserts in the United States." *International Journal of Environmental Research and Public Health.* 14(11):1366. DOI: 10.3390/ijerph14111366

Diamond, Jared. (1987). "The Worst Mistake in the History of the Human Race." *Discover Magazine.* May, pp. 64-66.

Diamond, Jared. (1997). *Guns, Germs and Steel.* W. W. Norton: USA.

Diamond, Jared. (2005). *Collapse: How Societies Choose To Fail or Succeed.* Viking Press: USA.

Duncan, E.K. (2012). "The Naughty Side of 18th Century French Fashions." *My Fanciful Muse.* Retrieved from: http://www.ekduncan.com/2012/03/naughty-side-of-18th-century-french.html

Dyson, Tim. (2013). "On the Democratic and Demographic Transitions." *E-International Relations.* Retrieved from: https://www.e-ir.info/2013/03/22/on-the-democratic-and-demographic-transitions/

Edmonds, Molly. (2011). "Ten Ways the Definition of Beauty Has Changed." *HowStuffWorks.com.* Retrieved from: health.howstuffworks.com/wellness/hygiene-tips/10-ways-the-definition-of-beauty-has-changed.htm

Ehrlich, Paul R. (1988). "Chapter 2: The Loss of Diversity—Causes and Consequences." In Wilson, E.O. and Peter, F.M. (eds.), *Biodiversity.* National Academies

Press: USA.

Ghosh-Dastidar, Bonnie; Cohen, Deborah; Hunter, Gerald; Zenk, Shannon N.; Huang, Christina; Beckman, Robin; and Dubowitz, Tamara. (2014). "Distance to Store, Food Prices and Obesity in Urban Food Deserts." *American Journal of Preventative Medicine*. 47(5):587-95. DOI: 10.1016/j.amepre.2014.07.005

Gries, Thomas and Grundmann, Rainer. (2018). "Fertility and Modernization: The Role of Urbanization in Developing Countries." *Journal of International Development*. 30(3):493-506. DOI: 10.1002/jid.3104

Knapp, Pat and von Zell, Monika. (2007). "Women and Work in the Middle Ages." Retrieved from: http://sandradodd.com/sca/womenandwork

Korotayev, Andrey and Grinin, Leonid. (2006). "The Urbanization and Political Development of the World System: A Comparative Quantitative Analysis." In Turchin, Peter; Grinin, Leonid; du Munck, Victor C.; and Korotayev, Andrey (eds.), *History & Mathematics: Historical Dynamics and Development of Complex Societies*. KomKniga: Russia. Pp 115-53.

Loudon, I. (1987). "Patients and Practitioners. Lay Perceptions of Medicine in Pre-Industrial Society." *Medical History*. 31(1):104-7.

McKinney, Michael. (2008). "Effects of Urbanization on Species Richness: A Review of Plants and Animals." *Urban Ecosystems*. 11(2):161-76.

McNay, Kirsty. (2003). "Women's Changing Roles in the Context of the Demographic Transition." Background paper, *Education for All Global Monitoring Report 2003/4, United Nations Educational, Scientific and Cultural Organization*. Retrieved from: http://unesdoc.unesco.org/images/0014/001468/146807e.pdf

McQuillan, Kevin. (2004). "When Does Religion

Influence Fertility?" *Population and Development Review.* 30(1):25-56.

Mission 2014, MIT. (2014). "Desert Agriculture and Agroforestry." *Mission 2014: Feeding the World.* Retrieved from: 12.000.scripts.mit.edu/mission2014/solutions/desert-agriculture-and-agroforestry

Moalem, Sharon. (2007). *Survival of the Sickest.* William Morrow: USA.

Piepenbring, Dan. (2017). "The Prince's Perfect Poo, and Other News." *The Paris Review* (June). Retrieved from: https://www.theparisreview.org/blog/2017/06/26/the-princes-perfect-poo-and-other-news/

Population Action International. (2003.). "How Demographic Transition Reduces Countries' Vulnerability to Civil Conflict." *Population Action International Fact Sheet 23.* Retrieved from: http://pai.org/ wp-content/uploads/2012/01/English_version.pdf

Seguin, Rebecca; Conner, Leah; Nelson, Miriam; LaCroix, Andrea; and Eldrige, Galen. (2014). "Understanding Barriers and Facilitators to Healthy Eating and Active Living in Rural Communities." *Journal of Nutrition and Metabolism.* Vol. 2014 Art. ID. 146502. DOI: 10.1155/2014/146502

Shannon. (2013). "Paradigm Shift: Changing Standards of Beauty." *A Day In The Life.* Retrieved from: http://sites.psu.edu/rclshannon/2013/10/17/paradigm-shift-changing-standards-of-beauty/

Srivastava, Kalpana. (2009). "Urbanization and Mental Health." *Industrial Psychiatry Journal.* 18(2):75-6.

Tellnes, Gunnar. (2005). "President's Column: Positive and Negative Public Health Effects of Urbanisation." *European Journal of Public Health.* 15(5):552-3.

Volti, Rudi. (2011). "The Organization of Work in Preindustrial Times." *An Introduction to the Sociology of*

Work and Occupations. Sage Publishing: USA. Pp19-37.

Weber, Hannes. (2012). "Demography and democracy: The impact of youth cohort size on democratic stability in the world." *Democratization*. DOI:10.1080/13510347.2011.650916.

Zemeckis, Robert (dir.). (1985). *Back To The Future*. Universal Pictures: USA.

www.ingramcontent.com/pod-product-compliance
Lightning Source LLC
Chambersburg PA
CBHW070042040426
42333CB00041B/1953